Beer and Whine
and Other Bubbly Concoctions

By Betsy Snider Heuer

For my kids, Jeremy and Hilary,

My husband Jeff,

My mom Selma,

And in loving memory of my funny dad, Harvey

Print edition published by Mixed Metaphors Publishing Co.
Copyright © Betsy Snider Heuer, 2013
Cover design by Steven Katz
Print formatting by A Thirsty Mind Book Design

ISBN 13: 978-1492722168
ISBN 10: 149-2722162

1. Betsy Snider Heuer/memoir-humor
2. Jewish-Gentile marriages-humor
3. Menopausal women-humor
4. Life events -humor

If you're quiet, you're not living. You've got to be noisy and colorful and lively.

—Mel Brooks

Peace begins with a smile.

—Mother Theresa

Greetings

I have no idea how I ended up as a stereotypical Jewish mother. I was a child of the 70s, moseying along with no long term plans concerning marriage and kids.

Yet here I am, a canasta playing (I hate losing, but my mother told me that no one would play with me if I wasn't a good sport), weekly salon hair blow out (somehow I can't do my own hair anymore), hovering caricature of my former self. I wonder if it's too late to break out of the mold and become the edgy, intellectual person more befitting of my large-framed, progressive reading glasses.

I believe in certain universal truths.

Universal Truth #1: Tall, mean people have a much easier time in life. I have endlessly lectured my children on this, and they get it. Life is just plain easier when you're tall, and/or tall and mean.

I don't even know how to save this manuscript on my Mac without bothering my daughter in Chicago. Of course she isn't answering, but to her credit, she is very good about checking in every day. That way I can rest easier in the evenings, knowing that she is still on this earth. Since she adamantly refuses to be one of my 1,232 Facebook friends, I have no way of stalking her every move. She knows I could never resist the temptation.

My son Jeremy is my Facebook friend, but he must be screening, if there is such a thing, because I'm never able to glean any good info from his postings. Although last week I noticed some chatter on his page about a Vespa. He bought a Vespa! He's driving it to work! OMG! I'm worried sick about it but had to think of a subtle way to approach the subject.

I waited a day and a half before expressing my dismay, exercising tremendous restraint. I was in Boston and came up with an excuse to email him, but rather than begin the email with, "How could you buy a Vespa?!" and listing every potential danger, I discussed the news of the day, then nonchalantly signed off with, "...and if you get injured on the Vespa, it will ruin my life."

He responded, "Don't worry, I have a helmet," at which point I went ahead and listed every possible danger. A lot of good a helmet will do if someone texting or speeding might hit him (G-d forbid!). (That hyphen is there for a reason, by the way; a Jewish custom to avoid the risk of erasing or defacing the Lord's name.)

*Jeremy in helmet for Vespa
(only worn if no passenger on board)*

Nora No More

I never intended to actually write this story; I only wanted to provide the ideas, and then collaborate with Nora Ephron. Sadly, when I finally began writing, a news flash popped up with the heartbreaking news that Nora had passed away. I am beyond upset about this. I'm sad that her life was cut short. I feel for her family, and for the rest of us who so enjoyed her witticisms.

Ever since I read *Heartburn*, it was my intent to have Nora pen my screenplay. I'm sure we would have been friends. The friendship would have developed naturally once we began working together. I first hatched the idea to write a screenplay when I was 35, and the protagonist is now 58. It just goes to show what happens when you procrastinate!

Universal Truth #2: The world is a sadder place without Nora Ephron.

My Family Tree

Before I go any further, I should introduce you to my family.

Jeff is my 71 year-old husband, who converted to Judaism. We live in West Bloomfield, Michigan, a very nice suburb on the northwest outskirts of Detroit.

An odd picture with Jeff actually smiling

Jeremy is my 31 year-old son, an attorney practicing in Chicago. Same looks and dramatic personality as me, so he grew a beard.

Hilary is my 29 year-old daughter. She is a nurse anesthetist who also lives in Chicago. She and Jeremy are very close. She takes after her father and has a calm, centered personality—nothing like me.

Hilary and Jeremy

My youthful mother is Selma. She lives about ten minutes away. She's barely five feet tall.

Her husband is Jack, my "wicked stepfather" who takes wonderful care of her and is an extremely devoted papa.

Becca, my Goth sister, lives in Windsor and has an adorable ten year-old son named Louis.

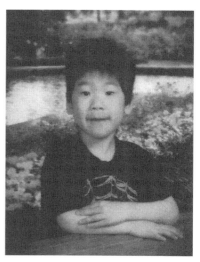

(1) My sister Bekka in zombie makeup (the ink is real)
(2) Her son, my nephew Louis

Jonathan is my 46 year-old stepson. His wife is Jean Liu. They live in San Diego, parents to our two adorable granddaughters, Galen (10) and Bree (8).

Meredith is my 43 year-old stepdaughter, an extremely talented photographer, married to Tom Wright, the nicest guy ever. They live in Beacon, New York, and are parents to our grandsons, Cleveland (9) and August (7).

San Diego Zoo with families of Jonathan and Meredith, including grandkids

Uncle Jeremy at Tigers Game with grandsons Cleveland and August

And finally, Ponce is my hairdresser and confidante.

Ponce - hairdresser extraordinaire

(1) *Hil and one long-legged niece, Shannon*
(2) *Jeremy and the beard (no escape, he still looks*
just like me)

Hil, Jeremy and friends partaking, drinking, karaoke and
dancing (They have wonderful friends)

Incognito

Back in the days of regular school (as opposed to Hebrew school, where it was obvious) I never wanted anyone to know that I was Jewish. I was so relieved and flattered when gentile classmates would exclaim: "But you can't be Jewish; you have blond hair and blue eyes!" (They overlooked my prominent, slightly bulbous nose.) Flash forward to today, when the first words out of my mouth let you know I'm Jewish and proud of it. I'm very ashamed that I did not have the chutzpah then to be proud of my Jewish heritage.

In my defense, who in her right mind would pipe up in class (in response to the Gurri twins' request that the Jews raise their hands, so that they could beat us up after school) to admit she was Jewish?! Also, an a-hole named Jerry Lill once approached me in junior high, slammed my locker shut, and spit out: "You know, you're a Jew, and you have a big nose." I mean, what's the comeback to that?

I just wanted to be built like a sturdy cheerleader with a small nose, at least *some* boobs, defined calves and thin lips. I had skinny legs, next to nothing in the boob department, the aforementioned bulbous nose, and big lips. And take my word for it: Big lips were not all the rage in the 60s and 70s. (The big lips fashion started in the late 80s with some Natasha Kinsky film.) Not to mention that I didn't even get braces on until ninth grade, when everyone else was getting them off. Another reason that boys didn't like me. I just wanted to fit in, and stop winning the spelling bees, where the winners were announced in homeroom over the PA system. It was not cool in my junior high and high school to be smart. I just wanted to hang out with the cool jocks.

There were no Asians or Indians at Groves High School, and I did not want to hang out with the intellectual Jewish crowd.

I was taunted in junior high with, "Won't somebody please take the lady with the skinny legs?"

One nice brave boy did ask me to be his girlfriend and gave me his ID bracelet. This was a big deal for me. However, one of the popular girls said that I wasn't good enough for him, so I had to give it back, and we broke up.

To try to fit in, I sneakily drank liquor in the ninth grade. We drank gin with orange juice, cleverly refilling the gin bottle with water. (My parents drank so infrequently that they never noticed the difference.) Don't worry, eventually I was busted and had to clean up my act. Today, I can't stand even the smell of gin, and I don't drink orange juice anymore (too much acid for my reflux).

Not to mention that I was only invited to *three* bar mitzvahs, even though I went to Hebrew School three times a week. Girls did not have a bat mitzvah in those days, so that narrowed the playing field to only boys, and not one of them wanted to invite me. The only three I went to were neighbors', where the parents insisted I be invited out of politeness. To this day I guilt my good friend Larry Nemer for not inviting me, and he's been paying penance ever since.

So, I was too small and skinny for regular school, for Hebrew school, and for playing outside with the neighborhood kids.

Helicopter Generation

A "helicopter" parent is one who is overly attentive to their children's experiences and problems, especially at educational institutions, named for the way helicopters hover overhead. The term gained much notoriety in the early 2000s as Baby Boomer parents over-involved themselves in their children's lives by calling to wake them up for class, or complaining to professors about their grades.

The cell phone is often blamed for the explosion of helicopter parenting. University of Georgia professor Richard Mullendore called it "the world's longest umbilical cord." In response, parents have pointed to the rising cost of college, saying they were just protecting their investment.

I'm not sure how my generation produced the first true "helicopter" parents. As part of the Boomer Generation, guys had long hair, we wore bell bottoms, and no one wanted to dress in designer garb or resemble our parents in any way.

Somehow I made it through school, studying abroad, applying to college and post college, arranging everything myself. In those days parents didn't feel the need to prescreen every teacher before their child entered the classroom. Neither was it necessary for parents to find a suitable college roommate by contacting someone's mother, who might know someone else's first cousin's father's good friend, who had a child with an acceptable pedigree. I've even heard of people asking clergy to step in.

At the University of Michigan, if a student is exiled to North Campus (which may as well be the North Pole, being completely separate from Central Campus), parents will pull out all the stops to get their little genius moved to the main campus. If complaining of severe allergies (the pollen level seems to be lower on the main campus) doesn't work, then suddenly this newly religious little prodigy (who previously skipped Sunday school whenever possible) will no longer tolerate even a morsel of non-kosher food and must eat all meals at the Hillel House (coincidentally located on central campus). If the kosher angle doesn't fly, this poor, suddenly religious little Einstein becomes ultra-orthodox and must be close enough to walk to services at the Hillel House. Failing all of this, the last resort would be to slap on a yarmulke and grow payos (the long, curly sideburns of the ultra orthodox).

Recently I learned of a new benefit in the Greek system. For the reasonable sum of one thousand dollars ($1,000) one can purchase a gold card that allows the holder to cut straight to the front of the line at Scorekeepers, a popular campus bar. After all, what parent would want their child to wait in line? Especially at a bar. Especially New Yorkers, and students who live with New Yorkers. I'm not sure if any gentiles are gold card owners, but I know that my husband, with his gentile roots, does not take cuts. (He does, however, seem to think it's acceptable to merge in front of waiting cars when driving, which drives me crazy.)

Hilary says that neither she nor Jeremy even would have asked for the thousand bucks if the option existed when they were in Ann Arbor. PHEW!

Adorable Jenna (Roz's daughter) sporting the invaluable Scorekeepers VIP Card!

My First Job

I didn't exactly relish my teenage years, but I did have a fun job working as a pharmacy assistant at Brown Drugs. Neil, the owner, was one of my dad's best friends and the two of them shared an eating obsession. He always hummed while munching on burgers as he filled prescriptions. I loved waiting on the customers, with one tortuous exception.

We kept the finished prescriptions alphabetically on a shelf. One day, a young guy came in and said, "Condoms, please." I thought Condoms was his last name. (My generation referred to them as rubbers in those days, so who knew?) I very sweetly asked if Condoms was spelled with a "c" or a "k." He said "c." I looked, and the prescription wasn't there. I checked under "k," just in case. Still no luck. I asked him if it was covered by Blue Cross (because we kept those prescriptions on a different shelf). He moaned, "No." I asked him if he'd phoned it in earlier, and he moaned "no" again. I then called out to Harry, the pharmacist: "Hey Harry, have you seen the Condoms prescription? I can't find it." Harry frantically started shushing me (by then there was a line) and ran over to get the condoms for the poor guy. He didn't wait for his change.

Fortieth Reunion

Out of a high school class of 688 students, only 60 of us went to the 40th Reunion. I went with three of my girlfriends, and we were the only Jews there.

Guess who wasn't there? Jerry Lill and the Gurri brothers were no shows. I recounted my traumatic experiences to some of the others, and my Catholic classmates were incredulous. One said to me that he couldn't believe that I still remembered both of those stories in such detail. I asked him if he was ever discriminated against in school for being Catholic, and he admitted that he was not. So there! It's hard to imagine discrimination without having experienced it.

I looked around the room at the reunion, and there was no diversity. The uniform for the successful, golf playing guys was: Navy blazer, button down shirt, khaki pants, beer in one hand, other hand in the pants pocket.

In all honesty, I didn't feel like I stuck out. Big lips are so much more fashionable now, and I was very happy to see the people that were there. We shared many stories (so many of us remember each other's parents and siblings), and it was a heartwarming event.

I was the only person in the room not imbibing, but I was very comfortable and predictably chatty. One person facetiously commented that it was too bad I so lacked confidence. If he only knew...

Anyway, I left feeling that I'd spent the evening with a group of extremely decent people, and I hope that (G-d willing) we can celebrate again at the 50th.

Universal Truth #3: It is important to take pride in your heritage, whatever it may be (with the exception of Nazis and terrorists).

The Beginning

But we should really start at the beginning. My mom was only 18 when she married my 22 year-old dad. Most women didn't attend college in those days; the main goal was to start a family. My parents tried for five long years to get pregnant. Understandably, by the time I was conceived, it was a given that the whole world would revolve around their firstborn.

My dad was sure I was going to be a boy, since his father was one of ten boys, and he was an only child himself. Thus, the stage was set for the arrival of a child that would be coveted, cherished, and protected from any possible harm, physical or emotional. The actors were ready, and I popped out on Valentine's Day, to further ensure that I would be the sweetest, friendliest little thing. The directors made sure that I was typecast as a people pleaser, and I was a natural in this role.

Eva

I didn't walk until I was two and a half, because my parents were afraid I might fall and hurt myself. However, I did crawl down the street talking a mile a minute. Thank goodness for Eva, our wonderful live-in African American housekeeper, who finally coaxed me into taking my first steps.

Eva lived in our basement, because our house was so small that the only space to fit an additional bedroom and bath was downstairs. She was absolutely part of our family, and we were family to her. Smokey Robinson and the Miracles used to practice in her house in Detroit.

Every morning, my mom told Eva her dreams. Then, using a sophisticated dreams-to-numbers conversion method, Eva played "the numbers" on my dad's shirt cardboards. I don't know what "the numbers" were, and I don't think she ever won anything, but she loved trying.

I learned about soap operas from Eva (enough to know that I didn't want to watch them). Eva's favorite soap was *Another World*. Every day at 3:00 pm, Eva watched religiously.

From this, I learned of several consistent soap opera themes. One is that there is next to no plot development. For another, after appearing to have been killed, it turns out that the main character was merely in a coma. After a year or so in a coma, the character miraculously wakes up, with AMNESIA, and a new face. Obviously played by another actor. (Since the plot moves so slowly, the original actor probably really did die.)

Anyway, then the new-faced character is reunited with his love interest, who in the meantime had married his son from another mother, who actually turns out to be the wife's own brother. There are also many baby kidnappings perpetrated by ex-spouses.

Eva stayed with us when we moved to the suburbs, where she had her own room across from mine, complete with an en suite bathroom. After Eva had a stroke and was in a nursing home, the only person she would respond to was my dad.

In those days, unlike in *The Help*, the housekeepers in Jewish homes (at least the ones I knew) were all treated like family. The families paid for their Social Security, health insurance, and stayed in touch with them and their families even after employment terminated.

We loved Eva until the day she died. I still include her in my nightly prayers.

Wuss

I wasn't shy at all, but I definitely wasn't tough. My parents never spanked me (in those days it was not called corporal punishment), because all they had to do was look at me sideways and I was already crying.

My parents were very involved and loving towards me, just not so much to each other. I was raised as the center of attention, but somehow this did not help me develop a strong sense of self. I gave away too much trying to please everyone.

I was raised to be very well behaved, polite, and by example to overly empathize with anyone who was suffering through anything traumatic. I was not raised to be honest with regard to my true opinions. I was petrified of getting in trouble, so I went out of my way not to criticize my parents. Once I told my mom that her hair looked a little windblown and witchy, and she was not happy at all. When this happened, I would worry incessantly that she'd never forgive me, and I haven't progressed much further in that regard to this day.

I never think that people will forgive me, and somehow I think that I'll end up abandoned and all alone in the world. Maybe if a therapist is reading this they could send me a suggestion as to how I ended up this way, when my parents always showed me unconditional love.

I react this way when my kids get angry with me (fortunately this doesn't happen often), or Jeff, my mom, or anyone else who crosses my path.

Consequently, my constant desire to please people turned me into a wimp. However, through the years I decided that I had to toughen up. I learned that I could stand my ground verbally and started interrupting people to get my point across.

Sports, Anyone?

I never considered sports as a youngster, not even dance. We actually played out on the streets, but I was afraid of most of the kids, and all of their dogs. We had our own dog, who was a very sweet collie, but I was afraid of him too. The other kids sniffed out my cowardice and naive, trusting nature. My next door neighbor once told me to go ask my parents what the word "fuck" meant.

Since I had fallen arches, the doctor told my mom that I should stick to Hebrew school and piano lessons. This was all well and good, except that in my physically underdeveloped state, I wasn't strong enough to open the doors to Hebrew school, so the other kids in the carpool made fun of me.

My dad took me to develop some door opening skills, and I finally succeeded. The first post-lesson Sunday, I strutted out of the car, pigtails flying, and pulled on the doors, only to have them stay shut. The carpool kids were howling. None of us realized that there was no Hebrew school that day.

Of course, this was nothing compared to the torture of riding the Hebrew school bus. I was petrified of the kids on the bus. The bus swung by several elementary schools in the area, which unfortunately yielded a wider circle of potential torturers. One boy pulled my hood down and chipped my front tooth, which now has a cap on it.

The torture didn't begin and end with Hebrew School. First, I had to get through regular school. I was the absolute last person picked to be on anyone's team on the playground. The only time the other kids called out for me was to try to break through the line in Red Rover. Ha! They knew I'd never push through.

I was also afraid of jumping on the pogo stick, and of walking on stilts. But I did win the entire 6th grade spelling Bee, for which I was awarded a dictionary with my name engraved in gold from *The Detroit News*. (Coincidentally, my father had won the 5th grade spelling bee when he was in elementary school and also received a dictionary with his name engraved.) I didn't mind being smart in elementary school, but this would change when I entered the miserable world of Berkshire Junior High.

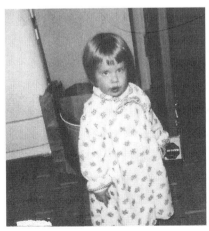 

Circa 1959 – Betsy   *Circa 1983 – Jeremy*

Sleepover Torture

I also hated sleepovers, and my friends hated having me, because I always called my dad to come pick me up. I hated sleepover parties even more than the dreaded individual sleepover. I did not like playing the Ouija board game; I did not like the levitation exercise, where one person lay very still, and we could pick them up using only one finger each; I hated sleeping on the floor, because I inevitably ended up with a bladder infection. Plus, I hated being exhausted the next day from having stayed up all night. "Other than that, Mrs. Lincoln, how did you like the show?"

The author with my mom, dad and cousin Mimi in Charlevoix, Northern Michigan

Pollyanna Syndrome

My first cousin Mimi, who is two years my senior, got stuck playing with me often, and she didn't have much patience for my Pollyannaish behavior. One time at her house we were playing "Saks Fifth Avenue." Mimi was in charge of the complaint department, and I was supposed to come in as the complaining customer. I marched in and told her, "I love everything about the store." To which she retorted, "This is the complaint department, you idiot! Don't you get it?"

Mimi has two older brothers, and they had a very cool little sports clubhouse up in the attic. Mimi's oldest brother Larry was a huge sports enthusiast and captain of the safety boys. He wasn't mean to me, but why would he want anything to do with his pain-in-the-ass emotionally fragile little cousin?

One day the Tigers were in extra innings and the bases were loaded, when Auntie Barbara (his mother) asked that I go tell Larry to turn off the TV and come to the dinner table. So, I turned off the TV and Larry yelled out, "Betsy!" (that's all he said) and I was inconsolable. He was in so much trouble, having upset his sensitive little cousin, that you could understand his reluctance to even acknowledge me.

In contrast, his younger brother Elliott would actually say "Hi, Bets." Elliott was the only boy in the world to say more than two words to me, so naturally I wanted to marry him.

Both his parents and mine tried to explain why it's impossible to marry your first cousin (without moving to Kentucky).

Pollyanna was my absolute favorite movie when I was younger. I even had a Pollyanna dress and matching hat. I'd wear this outfit and sing, "Oh beautiful for spacious skies..." I was a gigantic Hayley Mills Fan. I wanted to go to sleep and wake up as Hayley Mills.

At around age 14, I saw *The Trouble With Angels* and begged my parents to let me go to a Catholic boarding school. I was miserable back then in junior high, but they explained why a Jewish girl was not going to a Catholic boarding school. Plus, I didn't know anyone who went to a boarding school in those days.

Today, my favorite movie is *When Harry Met Sally*, and now it will only make me sad, thinking of Nora Ephron. I can recite all of the dialogue by heart. "Just who is supposed to be the dog in this scenario, Harry? Who is the dog?!" I also love the musical score. I considered casting Meg Ryan to play my character in my screenplay, but she's too tall. I'm only five feet two and a half (huge half) inches tall, which is really up there for my side of the family. My mom is barely five feet, and both of my grandmas were under four feet ten inches.

Vertical Challenges

All through elementary and middle school, my son Jeremy was one of the shortest in his grade (probably why he has such a great personality; he didn't grow up tall).

When he started ninth grade, he was barely five feet. I feared for his safety in the dangerous world of high school, so I corralled my Catholic nephew Tim (who was a very tall senior, captain of the cross country team, and a real sweetheart) to drive Jeremy to school for protection on the first day. He also picked up Jeremy's best friend Paul Chang. Paul was almost as short as Jeremy, and even worse, he was super skinny. When Tim arrived at his house, Paul came running out in pink shorts (I think they were Hilary's), because that was the first thing he could find to put on. Jeremy told Paul that he couldn't go to high school in pink shorts, but they were running late and Paul didn't want to change. Tim had his work cut out for him.

At the end of the first day of school, Jeremy told me that he wasn't nearly the shortest kid in school, that there were at least 20 kids who were shorter. So I asked him, "What did you do, count short people all day?" By the end of high school Jeremy had grown to a whopping 5'10. Hilary was never short; when they were smaller, my mom kept worrying that Hil would end up taller than Jeremy. She is 5'6. She takes after her father.

Universal Truth #4: Shorter people are more empathetic, having endured the torture that accompanies being short. Thus, they know what it's like to suffer discrimination.

Once in a while, I do allow for an exception to the "tall people are mean" rule, and my tall Catholic nieces and nephews are clear exceptions. They are all kind and thoughtful, and are very close with my kids. Plus, I really like my Catholic sister-in-law. Although we have very different political views, I have a tremendous amount of respect for her and her family. I always tell my kids that I know Aunt Karen would have hidden us during the Holocaust, because she is so decent and brave.

Still, I can't believe how on my side of the family my kids are considered very tall. On the Heuer side, they're the shortest ones!

*Jeff's dad Doc and my dad Harvey
(notice the height difference)*

Andover High

Andover High School was a fabulous school for both of my kids. I myself enjoyed their high school experience much more than I did my own. I walked down the Andover halls with more hellos and hugs than I ever received in the 70s.

There were two high schools in our school district. The Jews, Asians, Indians and Chaldeans (Iraqi Christians) attended Andover, while the WASPS and few African Americans in the district attended Lahser. Guess who had better sports teams? (Not counting country club sports like swimming, tennis and golf, of course.) The Asians excelled in school, and in orchestra. Somehow, their parents knew how to get them to practice their instruments.

Jeremy accused me of sabotaging his budding viola career. He never brought the instrument home, and after it was ruined in a flood at school, that was it for me. No more laying out another small mortgage payment to rent a musical instrument.

Anyway, Hilary was a "Pom" (basically a cheerleader), so we went to all of the football, basketball, and soccer games. We had a blast, but an Andover fan needed thick skin to survive. Our football team had some short, Jewish running backs, and the only size we got was from a few beefy Chaldean blockers (or whatever you call that defensive position). The football team played with a lot of heart, and our Poms were very good.

Basketball was a real joy for the spectators. We endured an entire season without winning one game. Our best player was a five foot six Indian named Rajiv. That would have been great, but our opponents from the east side of town towered over us, and we were routinely crushed. We did have one tall Indian on the team, but Ravi was so skinny that he fell over if someone sneezed. Again, we all enjoyed the Poms.

In soccer, there were some very fast Asians. You could hear their parents calling out from the sidelines. I don't know what they said, but their instructions were very effective. We actually won sometimes, and of course the Poms' performance was excellent.

None of the sporting events at Andover could have survived without tremendous support from the parents. The parents ran the concession stands, served as announcers, and provided sustenance for the athletes. When I went to high school, the parents were spectators, and were not in constant contact with the coaches.

Universal Truth #5: Jews and Asians are no competition for WASPS in the world of contact sports!

Another great Andover High School Poms performance

Harvey

My dad was *very* funny. I wish I could say that he still is, but he died suddenly at the age of 55 from a heart attack. He had blond hair, blue eyes, a round face and a large, booming voice. Since he was an only child, he was accustomed to constantly getting his own way, and he did not like to share his food. Maybe if he'd shared more of his food he would have weighed less and would still be here.

Harv was always on a diet, and his weight would yo-yo. My mom creatively hid her bakery cookies anyplace she could think of in the kitchen, but he always found them.

He was the pied piper of his friends, a real guy's guy. He was a great tennis player, having been the doubles champ since high school. Understandably, I was only drawn to guys who were good in tennis, and who had many male friends. (Unfortunately, this type is not always the most attentive and tends to always be out with "the guys.")

When my girlfriends slept over, he'd plop himself down on the extra bed in my bedroom and talk to us for hours. He once made a bet with my friend Laura, as they both tried to give up smoking.

When I got my period, he wanted to take me to his friend Neil's drug store, whereupon entering he let Neil know that we were there for "female equipment."

Tennis was just becoming popular as a participation sport again in the 60s and 70s, and my dad forced all of his friends to play, whether they were interested or not. He even forced his good friend, Sidney Forbes, to build a tennis court, Forbes Field, since this was not possible on our property due to some sewer issue. On any summer night or weekend you could hear him screaming, "Harvey!" as he'd miss a shot on the court.

My dad coerced his best friend Leonard into doing everything he did. Leonard had to: Learn tennis (he also made Leonard's kids learn tennis); buy season tickets to University of Michigan football games; buy season tickets to Detroit Lions football games; play in a bi-weekly tennis game; and attend any other outings that he deemed fit. Leonard would have loved to stay home sometimes, but my dad could be very persuasive. My dad had nicknames for all of his friends. Leonard's was "Gummy" (his last name was Goodman).

He was very opinionated, and he was always right. A friend of my grandparents' once told me a story about my dad when he was little. They were out to eat, and my dad refused to eat the main course. His parents told him that nobody was leaving until he ate every bite. My dad still refused, saying he would throw up if he had to eat it. They insisted, and he proceeded to throw up in front of everyone. Then he laughed and laughed.

My dad loved to visit our rabbi's house. Leypsa, the rabbi's wife, is a wonderful cook, and my dad once helped with an addition to the rabbi's home. He would stop by every day, and

Leypsa would feed him. My dad loved their golden retriever Samantha. The rabbi wasn't crazy about the dog, and Leypsa was always feeding her gefilte fish, chopped liver, blintzes, etc. My dad decided that Samantha could not continue to live at the rabbi's, so he told them he was taking the dog. They could come visit, and that was it.

When I went to school in Spain for my junior year abroad, Harvey said that he refused to come visit because of the Spanish Inquisition. How could he step foot in such a country? Predictably, he missed me so much that after two days they booked their tickets to come visit. When it was time to return home, he told me that he missed me so much he didn't think he could wait one minute longer for me to return.

When the Harvey crew wasn't playing tennis, they went to University of Michigan football games. Since my dad only had two daughters, and I was the oldest, he dragged me to many home games. He and his buddy Neil would overanalyze the game the entire ride home, while arguing about which of them ate more bratwurst at the tailgate, and who had worse gas.

I got very car sick from the whole ordeal. Believe it or not, there were no good delis in Ann Arbor at that time, so my dad would bring corned beef sandwiches for his seatmates. There are still a few of the original crew left, and they've never forgotten my dad or those sandwiches.

U of M had a very strict transfer upon death policy with regard to football tickets. Upon death, ownership of the tickets was to be returned to the University. My dad fought long and hard for his good seats (35 yard line, row 74, under the former press box). If he'd had a dying wish (besides not to die), it would have been that we not lose those seats. When he died suddenly, I kept paying for the seats.

One day, about 15 years after his death, I got a call from the U of M athletic office asking for him. I panicked. I said that he wasn't home. When they asked if I knew where he was, I said, "I think up north somewhere."

I frantically called my husband, who investigated, and determined that we could transfer the four seats to my mom, who could care less about Michigan football games (or any sports games for that matter). We still have the tickets to this day. The Big House is a beautiful stadium, and we think of him at every game. The seats are now in my son Jeremy's name.

My dad also took his nephews (my cousins) to many sports games. Their dad is a true intellectual and not a huge sports enthusiast. Every week there was a Michigan or Tigers home game, one or the other would call our house.

"Hi Auntie Selma, how are you feeling?"

"Good, thanks, Larry. How are you?"

"Oh, Elliott and I were just wondering if you weren't feeling up to going to the game, if maybe one of us could come and use your ticket?"

My dad was also a huge hypochondriac. He was constantly calling my poor uncle, a radiologist, for x-rays of one body part or another. When he had a hemorrhoidectomy, he stayed in the hospital for ten days. Eventually I convinced him to come home.

He said he was in horrible, horrible pain. He crawled to the bathroom upstairs to soak in the tub, while his friends were visiting. Then, frequently, he would drive himself to the hospital in the middle of the night, and my mom or I would go pick him up in the morning.

I had just started my paralegal job at that time, and the whole episode was very upsetting to me. One of the attorneys in the office had a broken leg with a cast up to his hip and was unable to drive. I frequently gave him rides. I would tearfully share the latest chapter of the hemorrhoid saga, and he was a captive audience, stuck in the back seat with his leg elevated. He said that he wasn't sure which rides were worse: Those spent listening to descriptions of my dad's hemorrhoid woes, or getting a ride with the main tax partner, who discussed the most recent developments in the tax code for the entire ride to work.

(1) Harvey 1944 (a L'il Rascal)
(2) Harvey and his parents (my grandma and Papa) in 1940

RULE TENNIS COURTS—Here are Detroit's in school individual tennis champions. Sherman Katz (left) and Harvey Snider (right), of Central, took the doubles title for the second successive year, with Bill Sayres of Redford (center) the winner in singles.

(1) Harvey and Shimmy Kaye (Central High School Doubles Champs) circa 1943;

(2) Leonard "Gummy" Goodman

Harvey and Gerry (Geraldo) Ingber

(1) Harvey and crew at "The Big House" - tailgating at University of Michigan stadium with Wolpin and Neil "Brownie" Brown

(2) Cousins Larry and Elliott at sporting event with Aunt Selma and Uncle Harvey

(1) Grandpa Harvey and my sister Becca (one of the eight short months Harvey was a grandpa) in July 1982

(2)Grandpa Harvey and Jeremy

Harvey in the Navy (circa 1944)

Romance

Growing up, I had a penchant for guys who were emotionally unavailable (but they were good at tennis!), in other words: Hard to get (G-d forbid I should make it easy). I started going with Rick, my first real boyfriend (but not his real name), while on an Israel trip in 1971. After the '67 War, summer trips to Israel were very popular for Jewish kids.

Rick and I started dating that summer at the age of 16. After going together on and off for nine and a half years, we finally got married. We'd been engaged for a year and a half. It turned out that we didn't have very much in common, and we had very different values.

Rick's main interests were: Suntanning, gambling on sports, golf, tennis, and making money. To torture my dad, he would start describing that day's golf game, hole by hole, until my dad would tell him to shut up.

So what drew me to such a person? Well, aside from the good looks (picture a mix of Charles Manson and Omar Sharif), he was a cool customer (he wore lots of velour turtlenecks in high school), did not act overly interested in me (huge challenge) and was intelligent, but not worldly.

He would plant himself on a chaise lounge and refused to get up even for a glass of water, so as not to miss a minute of sun. Now, from a distance, he resembles an Asian woman, due to the fact that following a skin cancer scare he now wears a big hat, long sleeves and long pants on the golf course.

Plus, he only liked me when I was tan. He has dark, swarthy skin. I'm blond, and very fair. Anyway, once the chase was over (and he pledged to love me even in the winter months, minus suntan), reality set in, and I was uninspired.

By then, I was working as one of the first paralegals in our city. It was a brand new profession. I'd majored in Spanish, following my passion rather than pursuing a more practical professional path. I didn't want to teach, I just wanted to speak Spanish all day long, and maybe become an interpreter for the United Nations (without having to move to New York).

In the meantime, my aunt mentioned to me that she heard about this great new paralegal idea, and although I never intended to attend law school, it sounded intriguing. As it turned out, this was a very good decision. I met interesting people, including my future husband.

I'd go for drinks after work with the attorneys. We'd discuss world affairs, the law, tell jokes. I was in my element. Rick had no interest in world affairs, and actually didn't like talking about anything. He was very quiet, especially when surrounded by interesting people. I was getting very involved in activities with our Jewish Federation. I was obsessed with anything involving Israel (ever since my 1971 trip). The Federation raises money for Jews, locally, in Israel and abroad, and I was constantly exposed to fascinating speakers and programming regarding Israel.

Rick didn't really care about Israel and harbored no fond memories of his summer spent there, since he had food poisoning for basically the entire six weeks of our trip.

I was married to Rick for a whopping eight months before we got divorced. I knew I wanted out by the honeymoon. I first broached the subject after being married three months, but he was too embarrassed to get divorced so quickly. We had a lavish, formal wedding with red roses, white glove service, a fabulous band, a huge wedding party, the works.

So, instead, I waited until the wedding albums came in, then put my foot down. Rick had no idea how to break the news to his parents. I suggested that he tell his mother that he had some good news and some bad news. The good news was that she was getting the diamond back. That's exactly how Rick presented it. His parents were always very nice to me, but that surely wasn't enough to keep me interested around crowns, fillings, and dental floss when I was constantly surrounded by people in the much more scintillating legal profession. (Although to this day, I am extremely diligent about flossing every night before bed.)

We divided up the gifts according to whether they were given by friends of the bride or groom. I was even willing to let him have the white Formica bedroom set (Formica was very popular back then), but Rick's mother felt that white was not good for his future bachelor pad.

Rick is still a dentist, and there are currently huge

billboards of him along several freeways. On the billboards, he has superwhite teeth, and there is language indicating that his office was voted number one! (By his employees.) He also drives a Bentley and is currently on his third wife, who is much younger (and actually seems very nice). I did write to Rick for a while when he had fallen on hard times. We had a very nice correspondence going—more than we had ever communicated in the entire history of our relationship.

Gotta love those Seventies! (1972)

Refills?

One advantage of marrying a gentile who converts is the benefit of observing people who see the glass as half full. On my side, the glass is completely empty. I come from a long line of worriers. After I was born, my sweet maternal grandma Berry insisted that there be a double dutch door to my bedroom, to stop the gentile family collie from attacking me.

Grandma Berry always worried about her family's safety. One evening, after leaving her parents' house, my mom, instead of driving straight home and reporting to her mother, took me (a toddler at the time) and Eva to the drive-in right near our house.

Frantic with worry, my grandma called nonstop until my mom finally returned after the movie. My mom was in big trouble. My grandma then called my auntie Barbara (her daughter-in-law), in tears. "What's wrong, Mom?"

"It's Selma."

"What happened to Selma?"

"She left and took Betsy with her."

"What do you mean she left? She must have had a reason to leave the house. I'm sure they're fine."

"SHE TOOK BETSY TO THE DRIVE-IN!"

"Alone? Or did Eva go with them?"

"Eva was also there, but how could she take a child to the drive-in?"

Needless to say, my aunt was very relieved that my mother hadn't run off with me to Afghanistan.

The first thing my grandma asked my mother after she got home was if there were any other Jewish people at the drive-in. (As if this would be very easy to determine without walking from car to car and taking a poll.)

I never stepped on a sidewalk crack so that (G-d forbid) nothing bad would ever happen to my parents. If they were five minutes late, I was frantic with worry. To this day, I'm afraid to ever fully enjoy anything for fear that some horrific tragedy lurks right around the corner.

If I haven't checked in with my mother, her response is: "I didn't hear from you. How do you know nothing awful happened?" (Please don't misconstrue. I'm extremely grateful to still have my mother, and I love her with all my heart. Plus, she'll be reading this.) This has been passed down through the generations, so she comes by it naturally.

Conversely, my in-laws, who had many serious health issues at the end of their lives, were happy with barely one phone call a week, and everything was always "just great." One year, on their drive down to Florida, we called to ask about the trip. They said it was fine, uneventful. Imagine our surprise when we found out that my mother-in-law ended up in the hospital in Georgia. To them, it was not even worth a mention.

Several years later, my father-in-law was driving to

Columbus and hit the median (you try getting a stubborn 90 year-old to stop driving). He was bleeding, and bystanders called EMS, but no way was he sharing that information with us. He said that his ride down was "just fine." He hightailed out of there before EMS arrived, and we only found out because the EMS driver called my husband.

When Jews have health issues (which are discussed much more frequently than is the case with gentiles), the entire family is involved and must move mountains to show their concern and interest. Hospital visits are mandatory for all good friends and relatives. At the end of my father-in-law's life, I would go visit him at the nursing home almost every day. He kept telling Jeff that it wasn't necessary, but Jeff explained that I actually wanted to go. That's how I was raised.

Hypochondria

I am a *huge* hypochondriac, but I didn't stand a chance of developing otherwise. My dad was very dramatic about every real or imagined illness. My mom has never experienced a day without complaining about some ailment.

My stepson Jonathan is extremely stoic (not raised Jewish). I asked him how he could keep picking up his daughters to play when his back was killing him. He told me that no one is really interested in hearing people complain.

This was a revolutionary idea to me, so I tried it out and lasted ONE WHOLE HOUR! Withholding complaints was exhausting, and it took every bit of my self control. I need to strive for another goal.

My daughter Hilary is very stoic. She recently returned from a trip with a fever and rashes all over her hands and feet. My friend Jodi stopped by for a quick visit while I was out, and I asked for her opinion about Hilary's rashes. Jodi said that Hilary never mentioned any rashes. *What kind of person doesn't mention a rash?* That would be the first thing out of my mouth, especially since Jodi went to med school for two years. Hilary takes after her father.

No plain headaches for me, NO sir. It's always, "My head is pounding!" Jeff suggests taking aspirin. My response: "It's too late, my sinuses are already killing me and making me nauseous." I'm never just tired, but "extremely exhausted and my legs ache." I get about a hundred hot flashes a day. (Jeff had never even heard of them before. His mother never had any, or at least never complained about them. Go figure.)

I announce my hot flashes with dramatic flair, grabbing even a cocktail napkin to use as a fan. I yell out, "Hot flash!" and the whole restaurant knows I'm "shvitzing like a chazzer" (sweating like a pig). I attend many meetings and fundraisers where we're all given plastic clip-on name tags. Did you know that these name tags also double as hot flash fans? What an amazing discovery that was. They're easy to pin on and remove, so it's a very handy item. Since I didn't invent them, I don't think I can patent their usage as fans.

I also announce when I'm "dizzy," and Jeff replies that I'm "always dizzy."

I'm extremely suggestive to all symptoms from any illness. I just got a flu shot with the inactive virus. Within five minutes, I felt the flu coming on. I know this is not a potential side effect, but the symptoms felt real.

In the meantime, even my internist thinks I'm a hypochondriac. Once I was in the office, and another patient was experiencing chest pain. My doctor said, "Now see, there is someone who is really sick." If I can't even complain to my doctor, who am I supposed to complain to?!

Recently I had a checkup and discovered a new condition that stems from talking too much without taking breaks. My voice has become very hoarse from a combination of acid reflux and allergy drainage. I know this because both the allergist and ENT doctor came up with the same diagnosis. As a result, when I am at an event and have to talk over the crowd, I start to feel sick from a lack of air. Neither the allergist nor the ENT were able to cure me.

However, my brilliant internist gave me a lengthy explanation about lack of CO_2 and oxygen levels, and he came up with a treatment plan. First, I have to speak using periods at the end of my sentences. This, he explained, will slow me down and allow me to take breaths in between (only I keep forgetting to try, given my penchant for non-stop chatter). He also suggested that I take a paper bag with me to large events and breathe into it when I start to feel woozy. Does he really think I can fit a brown paper bag into a Judith Leiber cocktail purse?

Anyway, I did try that the other day, after entertaining a houseguest (which requires a tremendous amount of conversation), and aside from smearing my lipstick, it seemed to help!

Okay, I may have been a bit hasty referring to my internist as "brilliant." After hosting Israeli houseguests for a week straight, I had a horrible case of laryngitis that seemed to be lasting forever and I wasn't sure if I should go to the internist or the allergist. Luckily for the internist, I decided on him and called his house at 7:45 am to see if I should come in. I was overdue for a fasting cholesterol blood test anyway, so I could kill two birds with one stone (and justify calling him at such an early hour). I had never called him at home before, but I was getting desperate.

After the examination, he told me to try not to talk so much (he always tells me this), drink lots of fluids, and use steam. Three days later, I still had laryngitis (I couldn't quite manage not speaking totally; laryngitis is so isolating), I still felt crappy, and it was painful.

Since it was a Saturday, the office was closed, but I was too uncomfortable to sleep, and I didn't want to wait until Monday to get started on the healing process. So, I got up my nerve and decided to text him. (I felt that texting was much less intrusive than actually calling.) Anyway, it turns out that he was playing in the same golf tournament as Jeff that morning. I realized that there was a chance my doctor might laughingly show the text to his friends, but I took a chance since I was pretty sure that would be a HIPAA violation.

I sent him the following text: "Hi Danny, sorry to bother you, don't know if you're playing in the Member-Member (golf tournament). Anyway, my throat is no better, and it's been six days; it's the worst in the mornings. Darlene (his assistant) said my blood work is fine except the cholesterol. She didn't know about the throat culture, and anyway it made me gag so much I don't know if it would be accurate. So it's almost noon, I've been drinking lots of fluids; throat still hurts, bags under my eyes; and how long am I supposed to barely talk? The cough is not frequent, and tight, and hurts through the ears.

Any suggestions? This is my busy season with the Israeli campers, so I can't afford to be voiceless. Plus it's boring. Thanks for any suggestions. Also, I was not going to take the Mucinex today because I think it makes me more tired. Thanks again! (sunshine emoticon) Betsy"

Well, Danny had the nerve to tell Jeff (on the golf course) that this was the longest text he had ever received, and that I should drink more fluids. That's it. And he didn't call. Or text me back. He's probably planning to change his cell phone number now. (I really need to find a doctor I'm comfortable calling, texting and emailing.)

I feel like I disappear when I have laryngitis. I realize that people find it humorous when a chatty person can't talk, but when I have no voice I may as well be invisible. As I was healing, I would speak very softly and deliberately. Some friends remarked that they liked this style. Well that's nice, but it's not my style, and it makes me feel like a fraud. I am not a soft spoken, overly polite, non-interrupting, always-listening-to-others person. And, contrary to popular opinion, that's not who I want to be. During the voiceless periods, I can't use any expression in my voice; it puts more strain on my vocal chords. Not to mention, I can't swear at all. (Swearing puts a tremendous strain on the vocal chords.) I am now going to a speech pathologist for further instruction on proper speaking techniques.

The following is a detailed list of instructions he gave me for Vocal Hygiene and Rehabilitation:

1. No Screaming, Yelling or Shouting (*How else am I supposed to communicate?!* Swearing is out of the question, and what about communicating with Jeff? All we do is yell. Oy! I was given a plastic clapper to get his attention, but he isn't responding well to it. It's like calling a dog, and he doesn't like to be ordered around.)

2. No Whispering (Okay, I can try that.)

3. No Smoking (No biggie.)

4. No Drinking of Alcohol (Again, no problem for me.)

5. No Singing (*Are you kidding me?* What good are iTunes, my iPod and Sirius radio if I can't sing along?)

6. Cut Down on Amount of Talking by 20% (This has been difficult.)

7. Use Quiet (Soft) Voice (I don't have a quiet, soft voice. The doctor said to imitate Marilyn Monroe. I don't care for Marilyn Monroe, though I did love the TV series "Smash," which of course is now off the air.)

8. Use Breathy Voice (Half voice/half whisper) (Oh, come on, like I have a breathy voice!)

9. Periods of Vocal Rest Throughout the Day (I've been doing that; it's extremely boring.)

10. Limit/Modify Telephone Use (No Bluetooth; use texting.) (Oh boy, I can't text and drive, and now I'm not allowed use the Bluetooth.)

11. Use Facial Steam twice daily (I've used it twice and it made my forehead break out.)

12. D.T.T.A.Y.C.T. (Which stands for "don't talk to anyone you can't touch." Now I'm acting like a weirdo, going right up to someone and sticking out my arm to see if they're close enough before I address them with my breathy voice.)

13. Avoid Noisy Places (There goes the party! I've spent the last month avoiding noisy places. Every restaurant is noisy. It's very hard to remain sociable under these circumstances.)

I explained to the doctor that it would be extremely difficult for me to change my entire personality at almost 60 years of age, and he assured me that it was possible for me to express myself in a much softer manner without changing from Jekyll to Hyde. I remain unconvinced.

So far, the only positive is that I decided I shouldn't golf or go walking with friends, because I'd be too tempted to talk to people who are more than an arm's length away.

I realize that (thank goodness) this is not a death sentence, and things could be much worse. But so far, I'm not enjoying the new me.

I was raised to believe that complaining was a virtue. Jeff was raised that complaining was a vice. I get a stiff neck just thinking about it.

Universal Truth #6: Jews Complain about health and money; gentiles pull themselves up by their bootstraps, and zip it.

Yiddish

We didn't speak Yiddish in my house when I was growing up, but it's the perfect language for a drama queen. It's so expressive and vibrant.

The word Yiddish means "Jewish." It was first spoken in the tenth or eleventh century among Jews living along the banks of the Rhine River. The more distinct their communities became, the more their spoken language differentiated itself from that of their non-Jewish German speaking neighbors. Yiddish uses the Hebrew alphabet and derives as much as 20 percent of its vocabulary from Hebrew and Aramaic. When Jews were expelled from western European countries, many emigrated eastward and picked up new influences from local Slavic languages.

These Yiddish speaking settlers are the ancestors of the majority of today's American Jews. Between the Holocaust and Stalin's Russia, Yiddish nearly became extinct. Lately, however, it seems to have experienced a bit of a renaissance.

Following are some of my favorite Yiddish expressions:

Oy gevult (Oh dear!)
Gevulte shmaltz (My own concoction, useful when receiving bad cards in canasta)

In my guntzen leben (In my whole life!)

Shvitzing like a chazzer (Sweating like a pig)

Shtup (Having sex)

Goyim (Non-Jews)

Tush (If you don't know this one, I'm not telling.)

Gesundheit (Bless you!)

Mazel tov! (Congratulations; literally, "good luck")

Bubele (Darling, sweetie)

Kvetch (Complain in a whiny way) (I'm very good at this.)

Shtick (Someone's specialty)

Schlep (To carry)

Schmaltzy (Dramatic)

Spiel (Someone's sell job, as in: "I had to listen to the whole spiel!")

Nu? (So?)

Mitzvah (Good deed; literally, "commandment")

Mensch (Nice guy)

Putz (Idiot; literally, "penis")

Schmuck (Jerk; literally, "foreskin")

Kinehora (Poopoo, a curse in reverse)

Ahftseloches (Just my luck!)

Chutzpah (Colossal nerve)

Farputst (All dressed up)

Farmisht (Confused)

Tzihitz (Even more confused)

Farklempt (Cocked up)

Meshugana (Crazy; abb. meshuggie)

Nosh (Snack; can be used as either a noun or a verb)

Plotz (To feel so tired or excited that you could fall over!)

Schmooze (Chat)

The following is a simulated conversation utilizing some Yiddishisms:

"*Oy!* It's so hot out today, I'm *shvitzing like a chazzer*! *In my guntzen leben* I've never felt such humidity! My underwear is sticking to my *tush*!"

"Stop *kvetching* or I'm going to *shtup* someone else."

"You are such a *putz*. Where is the *mensch* I married?"

"That *schmuck* is sick of your *spiel* and is willing to *schlep* to the neighbors, either for a quick *shtup* or just to *schmooze* a bit. Anything is better than listening to you!"

"That's it. I'm calling Roz."

"*Nu?* That *schmuck* is driving me *meshugganeh*!"

"Oh *bubele*, you know you'll make up later with a little *shtup*." (She sneezes)

"*Gesundhei*t! I hope you're not coming down with something."

"It's nothing. By the way, Adam got the job offer."

"*Mazel Tov*! Another lawyer in the family!"

"I'm so tired from watching the Olympics I could *plotz*!"

"Maybe you need a quick *nosh* before you have to get all *farputst* to go to the event tonight. I'm so *farmisht* I can't remember where the meeting is!"

"*Kinehora*, as long as everyone's healthy!"

Universal Truth #7: Yiddish is a very expressive language.

Getting the Get

So, how did I end up married to a lapsed Presbyterian, alcohol drinking, converted husband? Well, it's a good old fashioned love story: I got knocked up. Yep, Jeremy is our love child.

Building on mild office flirtations, my relationship with Jeff developed in earnest after a fight on St. Patrick's Day. It was past 5:00 pm, and a few of us were chatting and laughing in the office. Jeff came barreling in, and told me (just me, not the others) that I was making too much noise, and there could have been clients still around (there weren't any).

The next day I went into Jeff's office and told him I thought he was rude to me and that he should apologize. He refused (It turns out that Jeff hates apologizing), so I gave him the silent treatment. I think it had a real impact. After a week of what I'm sure must have been torture (or possibly relief) for him, he finally spit out a half-hearted apology.

A few months later we started dating, and the rest is history (a history of non-stop arguments).

After several months of dating, I stopped at Planned Parenthood on the way into the office. I received a call with the good news that I was expecting. I had to make a few arrangements, starting with telling my parents that I was knocked up and wanted to get married in two weeks. Jeff and I had been planning to get married several months down the road, but we were still in the middle of the conversion class.

Another slight blip lied in the fact that I did not yet have a "get" (a Jewish divorce). I had to call our rabbi (of whom I was very fond) and embarrassingly explain that I was pregnant and needed to get married ASAP. It turns out that there is a rule that a Jewish woman must wait 90 days after receiving a "get" before remarrying, to be sure that she is not pregnant by her first husband. (Of course, the man is able to get married the next day, but that was irrelevant here.)

My wonderful rabbi agreed to waive the waiting period and instructed me to get the "get" at my earliest convenience. He directed me to an orthodox rabbi who issued it from his home. Rick was very nice about accompanying me, because it is impossible to get a "get" without the presence of the ex-husband. I have heard of cases where the ex will not grant it. This can stop the woman from remarrying in certain synagogues and could even affect future generations if not handled properly.

Jeff was a natural star in the conversion class. After all, he had been on law review at the University of Michigan Law School.

The conversion teacher was a wonderful rabbi who was unaccustomed to having brilliant 39 year-old male attorneys as students. Jeff set the bar for the highest grade ever received. He knew a lot about Judaism, because he's very well read and interested in the subject matter. He had previously been the partner who worked on Saturday, the Jewish sabbath, and his Jewish law partners were not happy about losing their "Shabbas Goy" (a non-Jewish person who could work on the Jewish sabbath).

There are certain aspects of conversion that came quite naturally to him. After converting, he dumped the hedge trimmer and adjusted quite well to having workmen fix things instead of trying it himself. Now he just makes more of a mess in the unlikely event that he ever tries to repair anything.

Hilary once had no overhead lights in her bedroom for two weeks, because I couldn't reach the light fixture and Jeff was too busy to change a lightbulb.

He struggled a bit with the "sightings" phenomenon. He was unaware that a good Jew, immediately upon communicating with his spouse, is supposed to name off every person he's run into during the course of the day, and he must then repeat *verbatim* whatever messages were passed along. Sometimes he'd see three good friends at the grocery store and forget to mention it. It probably took a good three years for this to take, but he's now quite adept at conveying sightings.

Jeff also had to learn to report any new general developments to me immediately. Every time he tells me anything, I screech, "You weren't going to tell me?!" He matter-of-factly points out that he's telling me right then. So then I give him, "Why didn't you tell me sooner?"

Here's a perfect example: He casually mentioned to me

that the firm laterally hired a female attorney who just moved back from Israel. "What?!" I screamed, "Why didn't you tell me sooner?" I asked how long she'd been there. He said six months. "Six months! You know I love Israel, you know I love Israelis, you know I'd love to talk to her. Plus I know her mother." You'd think this would have been a no-brainer for him. Go figure.

Also, his "oy" exclamations have progressed beautifully, with an accompanying "ach" to demonstrate his displeasure with something. I can usually tell if the Tigers or Michigan Wolverines are up or down in the game this way.

Jeff says that humor was not a big part of his childhood. My father-in-law was raised in a loving, but stern fashion. As a result, he strove to raise his children in a responsible manner. My dad was so naturally funny and dramatic that humor and pathos were both very important in our house. I have a feeling that's what drew Jeff to me initially.

First Date

Since Jeff is thirteen years older than I am, when we first started dating I wanted to come across as sophisticated and elegant.

After the St. Patrick's Day argument there was a lot of sexual tension between us, so I kept a packed bag in the car, just in case I ended up going home with him after the bar one night.

We were out to breakfast on our first weekend date. I was wearing a green silk camisole and blazer with big shoulder pads (shoulder pads were all the rage in the 80s). Jeff said I looked like Quasimodo, because one jacket arm was always hanging down with the shoulder pad due to my narrow shoulders.

I lightly pounded the table during the course of conversation, and my fork flew into my camisole. I carefully extracted it while continuing my rant, hoping that Jeff might not have noticed. No such luck, but he married me anyway.

The next weekend, I was traveling to my cousin's out-of-state wedding. Jeff and I hadn't discussed exclusivity at this point, but it was pretty obvious that we were smitten with each other.

About a year later, we were discussing whether either one

of us had dated anyone else after our initial hook-up. Jeff responded that he considered taking out the woman he'd been seeing before me, since I was out of town. However, he said that for some reason his bed, especially the pillow, had a very strong scent of my perfume (Polo by Ralph Lauren, in the red bottle).

That's when I confessed that I'd read an article in *Cosmo* on the plane (I only read it when traveling), one of those "How to make sure he'll remember you when you're apart" help columns, that suggested spritzing your perfume on the pillow. I got a bit carried away, the top came off, and his entire bed was saturated with the scent.

Normally I'm not much of a *Cosmo* fan, but in this instance the advice was priceless.

I loved having intellectual conversations with Jeff (unlike Rick); he is so worldly and knowledgeable. This is great to a degree. Jeff has an intimidating demeanor. It was such a pleasant surprise for me to find the gentle soul within. Here my challenge was trying to bring out his softer side.

Eventually, I started competing with him when discussing various subjects. Also, after over 30 years of marriage, I've heard all of his stories hundreds of times. If we didn't share a love of humor, all we would do is fight.

No Jews In Grosse Pointe

When we started dating, Jeff lived in Grosse Pointe, a formerly restricted (against minorities), WASPY, beautiful neighborhood east of downtown that runs along Lake St. Clair. I agreed to move there with the stipulation that we put the "For Sale" sign up the second I moved in.

Jeff thought I was exaggerating when I said the place was full of closeted, drinking anti-semites. Sure enough, the broker was in the house preparing the listing papers, and he mentioned that he'd seen a local celebrity on television that morning, noting that she was quite good looking, "for a Jewish gal. Because you know Jewish people have that nose thing going on."

I turned bright red, and in a flustered tone, he sputtered, "Ooh, I hope no one here is Jewish, are they?" Well, everyone was (or in Jeff's case, almost was), but I thought it best to just sign the papers and get the heck out of Dodge. The neighbors were not very neighborly, and the postman had to hold his nose when he delivered *The Jewish News*. We moved to the Bloomfield area by the time Jeremy was born.

I should have vetted the Bloomfield neighborhood better, as there were no other families with young children. I was drawn to the house only by the decor, and the cozy looking

Lanz of Salzburg flannel nightgowns hanging in the laundry room. On the flip side, we had lots of babysitters for the kids, just no playdate friends.

Transitioning

I had a bit of a rough transition going from working full time to becoming a stay at home mom. I was extremely grateful to be blessed with two children, but I missed the witty repartee with adults, and Jeff was not around much.

At the beginning of our marriage, my step kids were still living in Detroit, and Jeff's office was downtown. If he wasn't at the bar with coworkers or friends, he stopped and took the older kids for dinner, while I was home alone with our little ones. I was so envious of other families with young children whose father was actually around. Yes, many of them are now divorced, but the grass sure seemed greener then.

My mom and dad loved to come play with Jeremy and would pretty much see him every day. My dad stopped by every night on his way home from work. He was so excited to have a grandson. He finally got the boy he wanted. (During my pregnancy he was sure that I was having a boy.)

Jeremy was only eight months old when my dad died suddenly, and I was devastated. I was the first of my friends to lose a parent, and between the adjustment to staying home and trying to cope with the loss of my dad, I had a very hard time.

I went to services every evening to say kaddish (the Jewish

prayer for the dead) for eleven months. I schlepped Jeremy on my hip and found much solace in this ritual. I didn't think that I would ever laugh again, but I looked around at the other mourners and saw that they were able to smile. There were three brothers at services whose father passed away six months earlier. I figured that they loved their father as much I loved mine, and they were able to enjoy themselves a bit by then. So I decided that it was my legacy to someday laugh again. Jeremy was such a good baby, and he was a great distraction for us.

In those days, conservative Judaism still did not count women in the minyan (10 men, the minimum requirement for holding a prayer service). Some nights there would be nine men and me, and the cantor (who chanted the prayers) would start calling around to find a tenth man for services, while I sat there like chopped liver. I did not think less of them for this, because they were interpreting Jewish law to the best of their abilities, and they were very supportive of me at an awful time. Today, women are counted in minyans in both reform and conservative synagogues.

My family and I are usually the last ones to leave events, including the synagogue. This drives Jeff up the wall.

Universal Truth #8: Gentiles leave without saying goodbye; Jews say goodbye and never leave.

Sweep It Under the Rug

Gentiles do not complain about money issues. For them, it's all about "sweeping everything under the rug" and drinking their sorrows away. Not only do we Jews not follow suit, we zealously communicate our problems to anyone who will listen. Growing up, we never sat down to a brisket dinner without hearing how much the butcher charged my mom this time. You could choke with this knowledge! The kosher butchers don't seem to abide by scales. They look at you, look at the scale, then slap on the price.

Kay, my mother-in-law (may she rest in peace), was a wonderful cook of gentile dishes (lots of butter, milk mixed with meat, casseroles, vegetables cooked in a pressure cooker, and so on). She was such a warm, loving hostess. She and my father-in-law Doc called each other "Mom" and "Dad". Doc always boomed, "Great dinner, Mom." And her response was, "Don't that make it nice. Can I get you anything else, Daddy?" If anyone was a bit too tipsy, it was never addressed. The Heuers all think they are the best family on earth. My husband thinks the atmosphere in his house resembled *Leave it to Beaver* or *The Donna Reed Show*. (Just add the alcohol and you've got the picture.)

After a few drinks, everything was repeated, but always

very lovingly. Kay never had a mean word to say about anyone. Both of her brothers were killed in World War II. Dinner discussions were frequently about politics, business, the economy, and of course the kids and grandkids. The more everyone drank, the louder the discussions got.

You could hear my father-in-law (may he rest in peace) a mile away, screaming: "ABB! ABB!" (Anyone but Bush!) He was an old school democrat, having been raised by a maiden aunt and grandmother when both of his parents died by the time he was a year old.

Doc's father died in the influenza epidemic of 1919, and his mother died from complications contracted during an appendectomy the following year. According to his mother's wishes, Doc was raised by his aunt Daisy, but was legally adopted by his grandmother.

Despite this inauspicious beginning, he was something of a privileged orphan. He, his grandmother, Daisy and a great aunt lived in a large and imposing house on several acres. This unusual family unit was supported "handsomely" by the income from a trust established for his grandmother by her father, who founded a successful ladies hat making business.

Doc was not a doctor, but obtained the moniker "Doc Heuer" from a friend who listened to the radio program *Buck Rogers in the 25th Century*.

Doc met the love of his life, Kathryn Lockerby, in the fifth grade, and they started dating in high school. Theirs was a storybook romance, and they were happily married for more than 65 years.

Doc was drafted into the army in 1942. His size (6'4, 236 pounds) and poor vision got him into the military police officer's candidate school.

His military career did not take him much into harm's way. Both of Kathryn's brothers were killed in Europe and her sister Helen's husband, Dr. Charles Van Gorder, was captured at Bastogne. (He is featured in Tom Brokaw's book *The Greatest Generation*.)

Doc was at Buchenwald after its liberation and helped organize the forced tours of the camp by nearby civilians, who denied all knowledge of the horrors that had taken place there, despite the fact that "you could smell it from two miles away."

Doc was a loving and devoted, albeit stern, father to his four children. He was less stern with his grandchildren (all fourteen of them).

Despite outliving his wife and many contemporaries, Doc made the most of his final years. His stories were a great attraction. The Greatest Generation label has become somewhat stale with overuse, but everyone in his family and many others who knew him will always think of Doc when they hear it.

My parents loved Jeff's parents, and my Uncle Harold, who is a true intellectual, had many interesting conversations with Doc through the years.

So, Jeff hails from tall, Scottish, drinking highlanders, while I hail from short, shtetl kvetching landschaftmen.

My in-laws Kay and Doc (1995)

Jews and the Phone

My mother-in-law never spent time "chatting" on the telephone. It was the exact opposite in my house. My mom loves to chat with her friends to this day. I love her friends. I'm very happy to go out with them. They're fun, interesting and make 80 look like the new 60.

One day, after a lesson on the evils of gossip, my mom and aunt decided to experiment having a phone conversation without gossiping. It went as follows:

"Hi Sel, how are you?"

"Fine, Barbara and you?"

"How are the kids?"

"Good, yours?"

"Fine, thanks."

"Well, guess there's nothing left to say. Goodbye."

Ordinarily, their phone conversations would last 45 minutes.

(Jeff hates when I'm on the phone, which really cramps my style.)

Here is one similarity between our families of origin: Large, lively family dinners with an abundance of food. Both sides would discuss current events intelligently. Jeff and I are both very comfortable in this setting. However, the preamble is quite different. Jeff's side has "cocktails" with the hors d'oeuvres and continue with wine during dinner and dessert. My side of the family only cares about the actual *food*; they could care less about alcohol.

Universal Truth #9: To Gentiles, the cocktail hour is almost holy, and is all about the liquor. To Jews, the cocktail hour is about the food.

Cooking or Not?

You'd think that I would be a good cook, coming from this environment, but the opposite is true. I seem to have counterintuitive instincts when it comes to cooking.

My maiden attempt at brisket occurred shortly after Jeff and I were married. I invited my aunt and uncle to dinner and they bravely accepted. I used my mother's brisket recipe and decided, quite logically I thought, that I could make the meat even juicier by adding more liquid. I noticed that my aunt and uncle were chewing, and chewing, but were nice enough not to mention it.

Jeff impatiently asked what I did to the meat. I patiently explained that I added more liquid to make it juicier. He retorted, "You made boiled beef. *BOILED BEEF.* You are not a good enough cook to improvise. You need to stick to the recipes." (Blah blah blah, details details.) He's so picky sometimes.

My mom feels sorry for him, because he was used to beautifully presented, tasty food. Now, he usually has to stop after work, pick up his own dinner, and cook it himself. Even if I offer to cook or barbecue, he'd prefer that I not bother.

I don't even think I'm a good cook. I could be starving, and whatever I make for myself is awful. Jeff's great on the barbecue; I'm not. Somehow when I cook on the grill, the food goes from undercooked to overcooked in the blink of an eye. Then when I try to remove it with a spatula, small pieces fall into the grill, and the entire meal is a disaster.

Currently I cook only three things well: Brisket (I now follow the recipe to a "T"); chocolate candy with crushed oreos and pretzels; and my friend Roz's bubbe's (that's what she calls her grandmother) mandel bread (like a jewish biscotti). I do deviate on the mandel bread recipe by adding flax seed, because otherwise I don't get enough fiber, and that can lead to another of my many ailments—constipation (another subject not discussed by gentiles).

Once I butt-dialed Hilary, and all she could hear was me talking to someone saying, "Yeah, Hilary and I are the constipated ones in the family." She was screaming, "Mom, Mom!" but I couldn't hear her. As I explained, she never complains about anything. Sometimes I just have to ask her about the weather.

Jeff's family did not dine out frequently, did not carry in, and barely went to the movies.

This next fact is so obvious that it barely seems worth mentioning, but we had Chinese food every Sunday night. After all, chowing down on Chinese food on Sundays and Christmas Eve is practically a Commandment. If Moses had received the Ten Commandments just a few centuries later....

So naturally, since I'm not a good cook and wanted my house to feel more homey, I decided we should get a dog. The kids were begging for a pet, and no way was I getting a cat (cats give me the heebie jeebies, and they're far too independent).

Jeff was not in favor of us getting a dog. His first response was, "Over my dead body." After that response, my mom said I'd better wait. Eventually I wore him down to: "Okay, but I'm not helping." TA-DA! I was on the phone with the Bichon breeder, and the kids and I, along with the pet crew (my dog loving friend, plus a Catholic niece and nephew) were on our way to the farm the next day.

I figured that we should get a small dog, since Jeff wouldn't be helping, and I'd have to carry the dog to the vet without breaking my back. So the dog shouldn't weigh more than 15 pounds.

We brought home Maggy, an adorable little Bichon puppy, and Jeff was not exactly on board. The first morning, Maggy planted herself right under Jeff's chest as he was doing his push-ups, and he bellowed, "How can I do my push-ups with this dog in my way?"

Two days later we heard him cooing, "Oh Magster, how am I supposed to do my exercises with you there?" He was smitten, a total goner. After a while, the kids said, "Hey Dad, we thought you said that you wouldn't want a dog?"

"I never said I wouldn't love her, I said that I didn't think we could manage the extra work with a pet." Yeah, yeah. We all adored Maggy, and it was the first time that I ever loved a pet. I don't know if it was because I was already a parent, or the fact that Maggy was so much smaller than the dogs in my childhood home, but I was mush for that adorable little creature.

Jeremy and Maggy *Gracie, our current dog*
our Bichon

Canasta, Anyone?

Recently I was at a fundraising walk for a wonderful organization that supports special needs kids and young adults. As we were waiting to begin the walk, I met two very friendly women, Arlene and Paula. Before introducing ourselves to one another, Arlene blurted out that she forgot to take her Prilosec before leaving the house. They then mentioned that there was no mahj game for the next three weeks. (This is typical conversation at any Jewish event.)

I can assure you this is not the case at a church picnic.

The card game canasta has become extremely popular again. Not one of my gentile friends plays mahj or canasta. I understand the close relationship between Jews and the Chinese. With our inherent love of Chinese food, it follows that Jews would also take up a Chinese tile game. Every Thursday at my house you could hear my mom and her friends clicking the mahj tiles, saying, "One crack, two bam, MAHJ!"

Canasta is a South American card game; I have no idea why it was adopted by Jewish women. I, of course, thought I was way too intellectual to play either game, but after retiring, I have to say that canasta is challenging and a nice way to socialize.

I've now taken up bridge, because my mom is a "life

master" and a very good card player. I was hoping that the card skill gene might be hereditary. However, so far bridge is extremely difficult for our group (still, I shall carry on with the lessons). Our bridge teacher, who is not Jewish, struggles in the effort to keep our group on task. If he lets his guard down for one second, the whole group is talking about anything but bridge.

Family Reunions

The Heuers constantly state that they are the best family in the world. For the rest of us, this gets old very quickly. I'm glad they're in a constant love fest with each other, but it's rather insulting to those who married in. After all, my parents and grandparents were and are wonderful people, as were and are those of my sister-in-law.

The Heuer family reunions were always a real treat in this regard. I felt totally out of my element (sticky carpeting, no air conditioning, no bagels, and obviously: *NO JEWS*).

The first of these reunions took place on Prince Edward Island where my mother-in-law was born. We went straight to the home of one of the relatives, whose husband was a Presbyterian minister. Since I was still saying the memorial prayer for my dad, I asked if there was a shul (also known as a synagogue) nearby; it was the first thing out of my mouth after hello. Jeff thought it was an inappropriate opening remark. Somehow, it makes me feel better if I can establish myself as a Jew immediately, and then move on to coexistence from there.

Universal Truth #10: Overly effusive love fests are annoying and insulting to the people who marry into that family (not that we don't still love them).

The Grandparents

My paternal grandparents (Grandma & Papa: 4 feet 9 inches and 5 feet 2 inches, respectively) were extremely devoted to us. My Papa would help me practice the piano. He was an excellent violinist and composer. He composed concertos about Israel that were played by actual orchestras (and he never even made it to Israel). He collected stamps, coins, paper bags, and always got up at 4:30 am to start his workday. He dabbled in oil paintings, and we have one of his earlier works (after 60 years the paint still isn't dry). He was also an excellent gardener and would fix up old houses in Detroit by planting beautiful flowers all around.

He made my grandma stay up to watch the end of Tigers games, and she would dutifully report the stats to him the next morning. On Sundays, Papa made a bagel and lox run, and he delivered the goodies to the entire family. He also sent me cards when I went to camp and college. He would buy them on sale, post holiday, so I got Valentine's Day cards on St. Patrick's Day, anniversary cards on my birthday, and so on. Even though they were slightly off, I loved getting them.

They called my dad "Junior." The minute the rabbi started speaking in synagogue, my grandma would stage whisper, "Look, Norm. Junior's snoring." We were very friendly with our rabbi, and he got a big kick out of this. Papa went to services every day and stayed for breakfast in the mornings, where the men discussed the weekly Torah portions, and life in general. Papa also wrote about the Torah, and I donated his writings to the synagogue when he passed away.

In addition to baseball, Papa was also a big football fan. He went to all of the University of Michigan games with my dad. We had to sneak five people into four seats in our row. So I'd go in, come back out with two tickets, then Papa would come back and sneak into our row. One day the usher asked to see his ticket. He patted his pockets and said, "Sons of bitches must have picked my pockets!" They left him alone; he was in his upper 70s by then.

My grandma was not as social as the rest of the family. Every day she came over to our house, whether or not any of us were home. She then proceeded to walk the dog, feed the bird, snoop around, and finally leave. Her departures alone lasted more than an hour. Sometimes my mom and her friends were in the house playing cards, and my grandma just went about her business without even acknowledging them.

My Snider grandparents, my grandma and papa

My maternal grandparents were another story. Unfortunately, my maternal grandmother died when I was only five years old, so I can barely remember her. I know from stories that she was sweet and unassuming. My mom was only 28 when it happened, and losing her mother was very, very hard for her.

My Grandpa Louis then became an extremely eligible bachelor.

Louis (that's what I called him, pronounced "Louie") was born in Liverpool (home of the Beatles!) with his parents having immigrated from Minsk, Russia. He had five siblings. Louis was 5'6 and weighed 165 pounds (remember, the shtetl genes). He bore a strong resemblance to George Burns, and was frequently found chomping on a cigar.

His father was a cabinet maker who worked in the attic of their home. There was never enough money, but every week something special happened. His dad would come downstairs on Friday afternoon. The kids were washed and dressed, waiting for him. He got into a tub of steaming hot water, where he would wash himself and rest. The sawdust, the thoughts of outstanding bills and collectors, they were all washed away as he prepared for the sabbath. He had a clean white linen shirt, black pants, special slippers and a yarmulke. Louis' mother baked fresh bread, cooked a chicken, and they had a rich, sweet, dark wine for the kiddush.

Louis was 16 when his father died. Overnight, he became the man of the house. They had to turn their small home into a grocery. His mother devised a plan for Louis to go to America and eventually send for his family.

In the meantime, shilling by shilling, they saved. Louis left, promising that he would send for them. Louis landed on Ellis Island in 1922 with $100 sewn into his underwear. He ended up in Detroit because he had a cousin there. He started out selling dry goods door-to-door. Even during the depression, he managed to save. He bought his first apartment building using $1,000 of his meager savings. Initially, it was very hard to get tenants. But on the afternoon of September 1, 1939, everything changed as Germany invaded Poland. Louis begged the bank for an extension. He believed that Detroit would become a boom town. It did, and inside of a few months the building was 80 percent occupied.

He would tell the story of one tenant, an elderly widow, Mrs. Cohen. Louis let her stay in the building even though she couldn't afford the rent (she only paid her light bill). After six months of free rent, the building caretaker told Louis that Mrs. Cohen was moving out. He ran over to her apartment in disbelief. She had all of her belongings tied together. "Mrs. Cohen, why are you moving? Don't you like the building?" She nodded her head, a tiny old woman, in a winter coat two sizes too big for her.

"It's—a nice building," she replied.

"Then why are you moving? Wasn't I good to you? Didn't the caretaker treat you right?"

"Oh," she smiled, "You are a nice man, and he's a nice man. And the building I like."

"So why are you moving?"

"Listen, Mr. Berry, I want you should know, for my money, I can get the same thing—mit (with) shower!"

In 1947, Louis headed a group of investors that purchased the Fisk Building in midtown Manhattan. Its tenants included the United Jewish Appeal and the Joint Distribution Committee.

The UJA is the major Jewish fundraising body in the US and was headed by his close friend Max M. Fisher.

The JDC devoted its energies to helping relocate displaced Jewish families who had survived the Holocaust.

The UJA asked Louis to intervene on their behalf to find more space for their offices in the Fisk Building. This he did, and so began his rich history with the UJA.

Louis got involved in some of the "secret meetings." When he was in New York, someone asked him to the McAlpin hotel where he got the whole story of the illegal immigration. At that meeting there were people from 20 communities. He found out from someone who came off a boat what was happening to the Jews in Europe. If they could buy enough boats, they could get their Jews out of the camps and smuggle them in. So they committed themselves for a boat. It was strictly illegal.

The Federation was against it because it would interfere with the campaign. Thus, it was done very quietly. They were buying the boats for $75,000. Louis and his friend Abe Kasle returned to Detroit and called a hundred people themselves. They got 75 people to come to a meeting and collected $1,000 apiece. So, Louis was already involved in helping the Jewish community in that regard.

They succeeded in getting several thousand people out of Europe and into Israel. Some were caught and sent to Cyprus, but the operation was a success.

The next year Louis was selected by the agencies as one of 28 leaders on behalf of the US to investigate and report on conditions in the Displaced Persons camps in Germany.

There were still millions of Displaced Persons living in the same "death camps" in which they had been held captive by the Nazis. They had escaped the gas chambers only to languish in the void of the camps.

Before Louis left on this trip, people came to the house

with sheets of crumpled paper on which they had written their relatives' names. They begged him to find any information at all about their families.

A few weeks later, the same group of 28 arrived in the British mandate of Palestine.

Newspaper reports of that day detail how they were shown about Tel Aviv under armed guard. Their plane was fired upon at Lydda Airport. They had been sentenced to death by Arab terrorists.

That same night the group met secretly with David Ben Gurion. Ben Gurion was the head of the Jewish Agency, a quasi-official Jewish government under the British mandate.

"We all knew," said Louis, "That within 90 days the mandate power would leave... and Ben Gurion's forces would have to seize control of the country if there was to be a Jewish State."

"Ben Gurion was a short man with wild, snow white hair and hard convictions. He was determined that he would head the first Jewish State in 2,000 years. His message to Louis was this: "Go home to your American cities and tell your fellow Jews and your gentile friends: We need help. We have men and women who will fight. But send us money for guns and trucks and the instruments of war. With your help, we can win."

On his return from Israel, Louis headed a drive for $250,000. "It was pay-up day, the day you had to give thanks for how very lucky you were to be an American, and how important it was to remember you were a Jew."

For the next ten years, Louis spent more than half his time on fundraising tasks for the UJA.

During the 1973 Yom Kippur War, although Yom Kippur is the holiest day on the Jewish calendar, the rabbis agreed that Israel's needs were so great that the lay people needed to take action. Louis and his friends shut the synagogue doors, made their plea, and raised substantial funds to aid Israel in her critical time of need.

In addition to the UJA, Louis, at the request of our beloved Rabbi Adler, arranged for the purchase of land and later the building of the current Shaarey Zedek synagogue in Southfield, Michigan. This was a huge task, and Louis was elected president of the synagogue twice.

Louis shared many entertaining stories with us. He was extremely generous to his family, and thanks to him, my children went to college, law school, and graduate school without incurring any debt.

He was also an astute observer. He had Jeff pegged as a real drinker from our first night out with him. Shortly after, Jeff rode the train to Toronto with Louis to a family bat mitzvah. Louis explained to us that Jeff drank the entire liquor supply (the mini bar bottles) on the train in the first ten minutes.

So don't tell me the Heuers are the best family in the world. I come from pretty good stock myself, and I'm proud of all of our families.

Uncle Harold, Grandma Berry, Louis and my mom
(circa 1958)

Louis in Palestine as part of UJA's first mission
(February, 1948)

(1) Israeli Ambassador Abba Eban with Louis (June, 1952)

*(2) Louis and his cigar in front of the Fisher Building,
Detroit, MI*

Safe, Shmafe (There's No Such Thing)

According to my kids, I have a horrific story of potential danger to accompany any activity, no matter how benign. I once met a very nice woman whose son choked and died while playing on the driveway with a rubber ball after it became lodged in his throat. Once I hear awful news about anything, it becomes ingrained in my memory for eternity.

This has also been a problem with my tendency to overly empathize with anyone going through a difficult situation, especially one that is health related. I get extremely upset when I hear bad health news. I used to obsess over it endlessly. I would feel so awful for the person and/or their family that I'd start to gag, which would then bring on panic attacks. Thank goodness for the invention of the Prozac-like drugs, because I function much better now. Not that it's easy.

Jeff absolutely can not understand why I get so wrapped up in other people's lives and stories, when their problems should not impact our daily lives. Easier said than done. Being overly dramatic and sensitive is a toxic combination. I have a hard time limiting my worries to those of the immediate family. If someone needs an extra hand wringer, I'm your man!

Say "G-d Forbid!"

I think it's very important to follow a phrase that mentions any illness or death with "G-d Forbid." I can usually get my kids to say it when I'm chatting with them, but Jeremy's been a bit resistant, as he's getting older and is an atheist (I think he's still an atheist). However, I will ride them hard until they spit it out, and I usually prevail.

Jeff, on the other hand, is a totally different story. First, as I've said, he hates being told what to do. He won't even smile for pictures when asked by a photographer. He can get one side of his mouth up. (I call it his stroke (G-d forbid) smile.) That's all we could get him to do in the bar and bat mitzvah pictures.

Here is an example: He was reviewing the trip interruption insurance policy when Hilary was recently traveling in New Zealand and her luggage was lost. He started quoting the "upon death" portion, and I demanded that he say "G-d forbid." *I mean, who wouldn't?!* He refused, and I had to threaten him loudly for 20 minutes before he finally caved, just to shut me up.

I'm trying very hard to have a more positive attitude. It's not easy, when my norm has always been to assume that something awful is about to happen to someone I love. I used to go to yoga to try to mellow out, but I hurt my knees. Now I go to Pilates, but it lacks yoga's meditative aspect to calm one's nerves.

Universal Truth #11: It's very important to say "G-d forbid" preceding any reference to actual or potential maladies.

The Barf Report

I also have an irrational fear about vomiting, aka throwing up, or "barfing."

I stopped sleeping over at my Catholic friend's house because she had so many siblings. The obvious result of sleeping in this environment was one main thing: Increased exposure to the stomach flu. I caught the stomach flu this way in the seventh grade and never slept there again.

If I knew my kids were exposed to anyone with the stomach flu, I'd stay up all night worrying that they were about to barf. If I heard a peep, I'd run down to their rooms with my heart pounding. Hilary's friend pointed out that the "throw up bucket" (an old pot) was out by Hilary's bed every time she slept over. Then, if one of them did actually throw up, I'd start gagging from the stress of the entire episode, so I wasn't very helpful. I can't stand when anyone throws up, including the dog.

I have great admiration for people who are brave when vomiting. I wish I could be hypnotized out of the fear. Unfortunately, I've made no progress and am still petrified of tossing my cookies.

Daily, I would regale Jeff with what he refers to as "the barf report," a detailed account of who threw up, when they did it, and where, within a fifty mile radius of our home. The barf report should not be confused with the "turdology" report that I would impart to him about the condition of our dog Maggy's fecal output. Jeff thinks I could have a second career as a dog "turdologist."

Accents

My mom accuses me of being kinder to people with accents, especially accents from the "old country." And I'm guilty as charged. Let's not forget that most of these people have stories that need to be documented immediately. Once this generation is gone, if left undocumented, the history of those times will disappear with them.

I tend to love foreigners generally, and I love to hear the details of their lives in other countries. I majored in Spanish and have a facility with languages. Therefore, I like to chat with gardeners, hotel housekeepers, and restaurant workers to hear about their lives.

I also love to practice an English accent—upper crust. (I have Sirius radio, so I listen to the BBC for daily practice.) My oldest, dearest friend Amy (who passed away from breast cancer five years ago) and I would endlessly chatter using our English accents (hers was cockney).

Our kids *hated* listening to us, but they sure loved Amy. We were so different from each other, but that's also how close we were. Amy was everything I'm not: Brave, a skier, a camper (she went on those river trips on pristine waters where you carried the shit can around with you; no way would I do that), an artist (I can't draw to save my life). Meanwhile, I was the only girl scout to earn *ZERO* badges. Amy's mother was our Girl Scout leader, and she really wanted to give me a badge, I just sucked at everything. Amy was non-judgmental, only liked nice guys, never mooned over a guy, never complained, could care less about trendy fashion, blew out her own hair, and was very laid back. I miss her every day. She was the greatest.

The beautiful Amy Dishell

I also had plans to befriend Princess Diana shortly after having children. We had so much in common then. We had the same haircut, we both had our firstborns in 1982, and Harry is only one year younger than Hilary. (The Princess was tall, but I was willing to overlook this flaw in order to take the kids for a playdate at Buckingham Palace.) This would have been the perfect setup, but again, I procrastinated, and Diana was killed in a tragic car accident.

Universal Truth #12: Speaking foreign languages is a blast, and even speaking with a foreign accent is worthwhile.

Haircut similar to Princess Diana
(never got around to that playdate
at Buckingham Palace)

No Snoots

Jeff has rather high standards when it comes to people with whom he'll socialize. He prefers the "intellectual type." My standards are much looser. I just don't like people who are snoots, and/or bullies. He prefers intellectual discourse to gossip. I try to look for the good in people, even if they're not particularly intellectual. I think that almost everyone has a story to tell and I'm interested in hearing all about them. It's like reading a good book. As with reading, if you don't like the book, you don't have to make it to the end.

The MEGO (My Eyes Glaze Over) Syndrome

I can only remember one instance where Jeff 's eyes didn't glaze over as I began telling him about a new person I met. We were in the Dominican Republic on vacation. I noticed a striking looking woman on the shuttle bus of the resort. She asked about the book I was reading, and (shocker) we struck up a conversation. Over breakfast I chatted all about Nini (I think he only listened because she was a real knockout).

Anyway, Nini came to this country from Sweden to be a nanny for a New York family. Upon her arrival in the US, the family did not show up to take her to their home. So Nini decided to become a flight attendant (stewardess in those days) for Swiss Air. Obviously many men hit on her, and that is how she met her current husband, Buddy.

Nini was on this vacation with her daughter and a friend; Buddy and their other daughter were off riding in Kentucky (they bred horses). Nini wasn't Jewish, but Buddy was. Buddy's mother did not like Nini and was always snooping around in her cupboards. Nini had trouble sleeping, so she wanted to borrow the aforementioned book. She promised to read and return it in a day. Buddy had been married before and Nini couldn't stand his ex-wife. When I finally came up for air (I tend to speak loud and fast, because I fear people will stop listening if I drone on for too long), Jeff asked me what Buddy did for a living. I said, "I don't know, I didn't want to pry." Jeff was so amused that he sprayed me with a mouthful of orange juice. The truth is, I really did wonder what Buddy did. I just thought it would be impolite to ask.

The other day, as Jeff was trying to ignore my phone conversation, he overheard this:

"You mean she had to leave town because she and her boyfriend broke up? And she had to move back to New York? Now he wanted a baby? But he wouldn't commit before? I can't believe it, I feel terrible for her."

He must have been particularly bored, because he asked me about whom I was speaking. "Hilary's trainer? You're talking about Hilary's trainer, whom you've never met, like she's your best friend?!"

"Obviously. What's your point?"

Interrupting Myself

I am truly afraid to stop talking when I have something urgent to convey. Sometimes, I have three important ideas to impart at the same time, and I even interrupt myself. Jeff hates it when I interrupt people. I agree that it's very rude. I'm trying harder to listen very carefully, then hurriedly share my stories before people stop listening.

Universal Truth #13: Gentiles do not interrupt each other as often as Jews.

Loud Talkers vs. Soft Talkers

When I'm with my sister-in-law's family, no one yells. Everyone speaks calmly, politely, and they listen to each other. Unfortunately, I tend to speak loudly (not quite yelling). When people ask me to lower my voice, I'm insulted. My mother always tells me to calm down. But I'm a very animated person. If I tone down everything then people would be bored even sooner!

Here's an example: At my sister-in-law Karen's father's funeral, one of her nieces, who was around nine at the time, decided to put on her mother's sexy, strappy sandals for the viewing. Her mom very gently said, "Oh honey, I don't think those are the right shoes for Papa's funeral, let's go find another pair."

If that were me I'd say, "What were you thinking?! It's papa's funeral, and you look like you're going out clubbing." I so admire Karen and her sisters.

Not one person in her entire family screams. They are so patient and reserved. As a result, the kids are all extremely polite, well behaved, and do not suffer from this generation's "entitlement issues." As my nieces and nephews are becoming parents, they are also calm, and I really try to behave when I'm around them.

Universal truth # 14: Jews scream more than gentiles.

Mr. or Mrs. Smith

I've noticed that more Jewish kids call their friends' parents by their first names. In contrast to this, gentile kids tend to refer to parents by Mr. or Mrs. This is also true of Asians. It took me years to get Paul Chang to call me Betsy. He was the last of Jeremy's friends still referring to me as Mrs. Heuer before I finally wore him down.

When I first married Jeff, there were some older people that I still referred to as Mr. and Mrs. We were out with one such couple at a fundraiser, and I had to just bite the bullet and finally call Mr. Zussman by his first name. Otherwise, my older husband would *really* appear to be robbing the cradle.

The Second Time Around

For some reason, I wanted an extremely intelligent spouse this time around. Although Rick was smart, he wasn't well rounded. Jeff is smart, well read, and an obvious intellectual. Although I truly admire these traits, they can be somewhat overrated. When he is embroiled in a deeply philosophical discussion, at times I need a break. I now realize that a person can be "smart enough."

Jeff is so smart that some people are afraid of him. (Luckily for me, I'm not one of them.) He thinks that I don't believe a word he says on any subject, and that I always assume he's wrong, but nothing could be further from the truth. I think he knows more than I do about two subjects: Law and world history. That's it. Oh, and world religions (he thinks I only know about Judaism, and that I clump all of the Christian religions together).

On every other subject, I assume that I know more than he does. This absolutely infuriates him. (He is used to people deferring to his authority on everything.) My mom thinks that we can argue over whether or not the sky is blue (we are both extremely stubborn, in case you couldn't tell).

I've come to realize that my feisty exterior merely masks a shaky core, both literally and figuratively. I constantly try to strengthen my core in Pilates, but have so far been unsuccessful.

I am extremely opinionated, and feel that I must always present my side convincingly and never give in. However, I keep reading that the path to peace and happiness is paved with listening, while quietly pondering both sides of an issue. These articles also stress the importance of letting go of the need to always be right. Like that's happening. (But I am trying.)

Anyway, since Jeff turned 71, I've had an epiphany. I decided that I should cut him some slack and try to be supportive, rather than argumentative (even though ninety percent of the time he starts the arguments). And guess what? It's working. We only argue maybe fifty percent of the time now! It's quite liberating. I must admit that I like a little excited misery every now and then, so I can't be too agreeable, but I feel much more mature in managing my responses, and I love the results.

Just married to Jeff (1982)

Jeff's (G-d forbid) stroke smile

Jeff almost smiling (Berlin, 2010)

Tourettes-Like Swearing Syndrome

Jeff accuses me of having terrible road rage. You should hear the stream of obscenities I spew when someone cuts me off. I get pretty creative. (The expression I use most frequently is, "You fuckass!") Although, when Jeremy was one year old in the car with Jeff and someone cut them off, Jeremy sweetly decreed, "That hasshole." So I guess that little ditty also escapes at times.

When Hilary was around 11, we were driving on a hot summer day with the windows and sunroof open. The guy in front of me stopped suddenly for a yellow light, so I had to slam on the brakes, and our dog Maggy flew off the seat.

All that came out of my mouth was, "You idiot!" Who knew he could hear me? He marched out of his car and started screaming obscenities at me in front of my daughter. I was actually kind of scared, but as he walked away I muttered, "Oooh, oooh, I'm so scared," then I drove very slowly, so as not to drive next to him. What kind of person screams at someone in front of a small child? And such a violent reaction when (for once) I wasn't even swearing. Jeff finds my swearing extremely offensive. Unfortunately, that isn't enough of an incentive to stop me.

If I'm playing cards with a more refined group, I start out

by using only "S-H." This is great, until I get crappy cards and the bursts progress to: "Fucking shit!"

I'm going for a sort of "irreverent elegance," if there is such a thing. I very much admire well behaved, soft spoken people. I'm just not one of them.

Community Theater

In fourth grade, Jeremy came home from school with the very exciting news that he was going to audition for the Bloomfield Players production of *South Pacific*. We went to the rehearsal, and he got a small part in the chorus. This community theater group is run through our school district. I went to all of the rehearsals and shows, and was champing at the bit to get on stage myself.

In the eighth grade, I tried out for *Bye Bye Birdie*. I sang so softly at the audition that I was not cast. It was agony watching the rest of my friends in that show. For my religious consecration I was given a shared solo part which, after auditions, was awarded to only three people. This somewhat restored my confidence, but unfortunately I had laryngitis on the day of the actual consecration.

After that, every time I auditioned I got some part. Following *South Pacific*, the kids and I were in community theater shows for ten years. I loved it. I learned to tap as an adult and frequently played ditzy blondes. Best of all, I finally got to be in *Bye Bye Birdie*. I was cast in the very fun role (in addition to general chorus) of Gloria Rasputin, Albert's temporary floozy. That was my breakout role. Bloomfield Players only produces musicals; I've never been in a straight show. All of these parts led up to my biggest role as Miss Gulch (and the Wicked Witch of the West) in *The Wizard of Oz*. I worked so hard and hoped that I might finally get noticed by the amateur reviewer in the local paper. Instead, he positively reviewed the other leads and said nothing about me. I was crushed. He had a son at the kids' high school. I couldn't believe he didn't like my performance.

I had to shove the poor dog into a picnic basket, melt into a small space where the techies pulled me through a box (at great peril to my limbs!)... So I stupidly called him to ask what he didn't like about my performance. (After all, my 88 year-old aunt, who attended every show, thought that I was going places!) He said it was his opinion that I tried to emulate the performance of the iconic Margaret Hamilton. (Ya think?) Plus, I saw little kids recoil in fear from my chilling performance. By neglecting to mention me, he made me question my talents. Fortunately (or not, depending who you ask) that didn't keep me down, and I went on to perform in many other shows.

I'd say my most interesting role was that of a lipstick lesbian in a play called *What's in a Name?* This was a show put on by the Michigan Jewish Aids Coalition. I interviewed several lesbians to try to get into character, and it was a wonderful learning experience. Every cast becomes like family for a few months, and it was always a let down when a show was over.

Sometimes people would recognize me on the street (okay,

two people, but still) and say they'd loved a particular show. One day, I went to rent a video at Blockbuster (remember those days?), a French film called *My Wife is an Actress* (I love foreign films). While I was picking out the video, of course I ran into someone I knew, and we chatted. By the time the long, greasy haired Blockbuster employee was checking out the video, I forgot which movie I'd rented. He started to say his shpiel: "*My Wife is an Actress* is due back..." Anyway, as soon as he said "my wife is an actress," thinking he was referring to the fact that he'd seen me in a show, I piped up with, "Oh, really? I'm in community theater, too." He looked at me strangely, and I did think that he looked too young to be married. Oh well. *C'est la vie!*

Bless You

In one of my many anecdotal studies regarding the differences between Jews and gentiles, I've noticed that Jews always acknowledge a sneeze with "G-d bless you," "Bless you," or "Gesundheit!" We believe if we don't say this, that (G-d forbid) the sneezer could drop dead.

I was in my brother-in-law's Presbyterian church when a congregant sneezed quite loudly. I couldn't believe it, but not one "Bless you." And it's not just in a church that this happens (maybe they believe Jesus is already blessing them, being in church and all). When I'm with gentiles, I don't say "Bless you" either, so as not to call attention to my nose and lips. When someone sneezes in a synagogue, the entire congregation says "Bless you." (The rabbi may even interrupt a sermon to do so.)

I checked with my Chinese daughter-in-law about the Chinese custom in this regard. She said that there is a Chinese saying when someone sneezes that references a hundred years. However, neither she nor anyone in her family uses it, so again, we're back to the Jews.

Universal Truth #15: Gentiles do not say "Bless you" when someone sneezes; Jews say it immediately, to get it in quickly enough in case the person should (G-d forbid) keel over.

Don't Blow Out the Candles!

Similarly, Jews insist that the birthday person first make the wish, then blow out the candles, and only then can everyone sing *Happy Birthday*. Again, Jews do not sing *Happy Birthday* before the candle blowout, or the wish won't come true. (OBVIOUSLY.)

On Jeff's side, they sing *Happy Birthday* as soon as the candles are lit. Poopoopoo!

Uppity

Roz has a beautiful condo at Bay Harbor in northern Michigan. Northern Michigan is a haven for the very wealthy in the summers, much like the Hamptons in New York. There are certain shops that cater to a particular clientèle, and that clientèle is not Jewish. When I walk into such a shop, I am sure that my nose grows two inches, my lips get bigger, and I'm immediately reduced to my former junior high school misfit.

I was in a gourmet food store where what appeared to be nuts were displayed in a beautiful porcelain bowl. I don't even like nuts, so I don't know what possessed me to try them, but I bit into the first one and it was so hard I almost broke a tooth. (It turns out that these were discarded olive pits.) The store didn't even offer me anything to pacify me for the aching tooth after it became clear to them what had transpired. I might have needed a new set of teeth!

There is a new shop in Bay Harbor that exudes nothing but pretentiousness. My friend and I entered wearing walking shorts and gym shoes, hair up, a bit sweaty. The shop manager did not even nod in our direction. We might as well have been wearing the yellow Star of David.

So I decided, as an experiment, to change into my preppy

shorts and sandals and comb down the blond hair, to gauge the manager's reaction. In my gentile costume, while slipping "Palm Beach" into every other sentence, I was given the royal treatment, including the history of the company, and even an invitation to the grand opening. (In fairness, the shower and clean clothes may have had something to do with it.)

Men

My mom thinks that I place much too much importance on looks, but there is a good reason for this. It's been my experience that most men are very shallow, and they place a major emphasis on outward beauty.

Last week I had a conditioner on my hair under a shower cap at the hair salon. Ponce said I had time to run out to Starbucks before he removed the contraption. I couldn't believe how many dirty looks men gave me. Not one of them held the door for me, they cut me off on the road, and I'm sure that if I'd been run over, not one would have stopped to help. A very sad state of affairs.

Of course there are exceptions: My son, stepson, step son-in-law, stepfather and Catholic nephews to name a few.

I could never be a bar rat; I just don't have the looks for it. (I'm still recovering from not being asked to dance in junior high school.)

Israel

After my kids and family, my biggest passion is Israel. I strongly believe that the mere existence of the state of Israel today is a miracle.

From my first visit at the age of 16 in 1971, Israel has been a part of my heart and soul. The majority of the charitable organizational work I do revolves around Israel and the Jewish Federation.

Israel's history is greatly intertwined with the fate of the Jews, following the Holocaust. The survivors (not that there were many after the Nazis murdered six million Jewish men, women and children) who managed to get to Palestine arrived half dead. Imagine leaving your country of birth, under perhaps the most horrific circumstances imaginable, having to work to make the desert bloom, all while learning a newly revived language.

David Ben Gurion listened to all of the different tongues that were spoken as the pioneers worked together and decided that there must be a common language. So emerged the birth of modern Hebrew.

In 1947 the UN voted on a Partition Plan that called for Jewish and Arab states to live side by side away from British-ruled Mandatory Palestine. The 650,000 Jews accepted the plan. They were outnumbered and outgunned, and could easily have been defeated by the five attacking Arab armies, including the British-trained Jordanians. They fought with hard to acquire weapons and eventually won, but at a great price. They lost one percent of their entire population. This was the first of several wars Israel would win to defend its very existence.

Historically, things did not work out so well for the Jews when they had no homeland. During World War II, the Jews were turned away from every country (including Palestine) trying to escape the Nazis. They had no place to go.

The entire state of Israel is approximately the size of New Jersey. Israelis are sick of war. They have a positive, fatalistic view of life. They have affirmed life in a way that is difficult to imagine.

Israeli politics are complicated. Sure, the same could be said for any country, but Israel is the only true democracy in the Middle East, and as a result, there are many internal political battles. Despite peace treaties with Egypt (1979) and Jordan (1994), and the withdrawals from southern Lebanon and from Gaza, peace still eludes her.

I've been to Israel 15 times, and although from three Israelis I may get three different opinions, every Israeli with whom I've spoken wants peace based on major territorial compromise and a two state solution, if possible.

Every time I see an Israeli flag billowing in the wind, I marvel at the miracle that is this wondrous country. It is so ancient and yet so modern at the same time.

My father-in-law thought that I cared more about Israel as a country than I did about the United States. I can understand where he might get this idea, but I have plenty of room in my heart to love both, much as I love both of my children equally.

Universal Truth #16: Democratic societies invite tolerance and respect.

Traveling to the Holy Land

On my last trip to Israel there were many orthodox Jews on the flight. Orthodox women dress very modestly (arms covered, long skirts, attractive wigs). When I travel, it's very important that I dress in layers so I can quickly strip down to a tank top at the first sign of a hot flash.

So as we're all getting settled for the flight before takeoff, I felt the heat starting to build, and—OY!—a hot flash. Off comes the scarf, the jacket, and I'm stripped down to a low cut tank. I'd been trying to behave in a respectful manner, but there's no negotiating with a hot flash.

Flights to Israel are full of chatty Jews, and not everyone on the flight immediately follows directions. There is a very strict rule upon entering Israeli air space that all passengers must be seated. The pilot makes this announcement well in advance so that everyone can quickly use the restrooms if necessary and be seated in a timely manner.

I remember a particularly long line when the pilot made this announcement (I do not understand what people do for so long in a matchbox of an airplane bathroom, they're gross.) where the pilot had to urge people to return to their seats three times before anyone budged.

On one El Al flight, per standard, the announcement was made that everyone must remain seated until the plane came to a complete stop at the gate. The plane landed, and up jumped several passengers to start removing their belongings from the overhead bin. The pilot came on and said, "For those of you who remained seated, I thank you. For those who are standing against the rules, Bruchim Haba'im: Welcome home."

Our family was once on a plane returning from Orlando with a Japanese tour group that had been to Disneyworld. The plane was silent. Everyone obeyed directions, people waited patiently in lines, it was unbelievable. Such a contrast to a typical flight to the Holy Land.

Leaving Israel a few weeks ago, I met a very nice Delta employee, a young Jewish Indian gentleman named Ravi, and we got to chatting during the check-in process. When Roz and Stanford checked in after me, he said, "You must know Betsy?"

Then, three hours later, Ravi was helping at security before the plane and we were so excited to meet again. It turns out that he's going to be placed outside of Chicago, where my kids live. Maybe we'll get together.

Jeff doesn't believe in sharing stories with people he doesn't know (it's the gentile upbringing). Once we were driving to Chicago to play golf with our friends. We stopped to get gas and, predictably, the line for the women's restroom was longer than the men's. While waiting I met some very nice people, and in five minutes I felt truly attached to three of them. Jeff brusquely indicated that we had to leave that minute, or we'd miss the tee off time (like that's a threat; I could care less about golf). I begrudgingly left the line, and everyone waved.

"Why are they waving at you? How much could you have possibly discussed in such a short time?"

If he only knew...

Drama Queen

Jeff cannot stand the drama when I read and react to emails and/or *The Jewish News*. As do many *Jewish News* readers, I read the paper from back to front, starting with the obituaries. Perhaps if I spoke in a monotone, my readings would not bother him. He doesn't appreciate my overly dramatic nature.

When I'm reading that Sophie Perlstein passed away, and can he believe it?! (It turns out he can.) Or that I can't believe that the Goldsteins have been married 50 years already (He also has no problem believing this.) or that Justin and Sammy are engaged (Or this.) invariably he bellows, "Not another dramatic reading of *The Jewish News!*" You'd think he could feign a little interest, but instead he stomps out of the room.

Jeff is very impatient with any sign of drama from me. Once, as part of volunteering for the Jewish Book Fair (a wonderful event), I gave two authors a ride to the airport. One wrote a book on Alzheimer's, and the other is a biogeneticist or some such thing.

Anyway, the Alzheimer's author (whose book contains an entire chapter on how to better manage stress) was very concerned that we hadn't planned to leave for the airport early enough, so I gladly agreed to pick up the authors half an hour earlier.

I thought this was a perfect opportunity to massage him for some advice on publishing this memoir, and to portray myself as a competent, interesting person. The minute they got in the car, the Alzheimer's author began studying his iPhone to be sure that I was taking the best route to the airport. I tried to assure them that I have a fantastic sense of direction, and that I drive to the airport frequently. As I was pointing out the lack of directional signage to the airport, Alzheimer's told me that I was going the wrong way.

Suddenly the freeway looked unfamiliar, and I was questioning myself. He insisted that I get off, turn around, and hurry, as now he was really sure we'd miss his flight. I complied, and immediately realized that he was wrong. I'd been right, and now I needed to recalculate and take another route. He insisted that I stay on the incorrect freeway (the other author was on the phone in the back; being more relaxed, he assumed that I'd get them there eventually).

In the meantime, I called Jeff, who was home with a horrible cough (that kept me up all night). Anyway, he is absolutely no fun to be around and a total curmudgeon when he doesn't feel well. He is, however, very good at giving directions. Since I called him for directional help using my Bluetooth, the authors could hear every word. He started screaming at me to pay attention to the road, and that he didn't want any soup (I had offered to pick some up for him earlier). Now the authors thought I was incompetent *and* had a psycho for a husband.

So much for exuding just the right amount of confidence and great sense of direction! Well, I got off and began taking side streets, reassuring them again that I absolutely knew what I was doing. Alzheimer's replied, "You'll have to pardon me if I don't have confidence that you're going in the right direction." The problem with insisting that you're good at something, screwing up, then re-insisting, is that the doubting party doesn't believe you the second time around. (Go figure.)

Of course I stopped listening to him and got them there with plenty of time to spare. Needless to say, I had no opportunity to discuss marketing strategy, since I spent the entire car ride defending my wonderful sense of direction.

Always drama—and the lips!

Parking and Backing Up

I currently drive a Honda Crosstour with a backup camera. For the life of me, I cannot figure out the purpose of the backup camera. It doesn't beep before I hit something, so all I do is watch myself back up right into the wall (or whatever else is in my path). For my next car, I need a beeping signal to warn me before I hit a wall.

Also, I've been having a lot of trouble finding my car in parking lots lately. This led to a great idea at airline parking: I took a picture of my car, in the parking space, with a picture of the pole indicating the section and row number. It was sheer brilliance! And it would have been perfect, were I not facing the wrong row when I took the picture. As a result, it took me over an hour to find the car. Thank goodness for the alarm on the car remote or I might still be looking.

Cleaning is Lonely

Jeff accuses me of intentionally making too much ruckus when I'm cleaning up after a meal. (There are still dishes to be washed when you carry in!) Plus, when Jeff cooks he utilizes every possible utensil to prepare the meal.

He shouts, "Can you possibly make more noise?" and exits the room. One day I managed to knock over a bottle of wine, and I almost went deaf from the crash in the fridge. Then I dropped the leash on the floor when I went to walk the dog. Jeff refuses to believe I could produce such a cacophony by accident. Our current dog Gracie hates loud noises, and she has to run and hide.

I find cleaning both uninteresting and lonely, so after Jeff abandons me in the kitchen, I usually put on my iTunes headphones, which further exacerbates our communication issues, inviting more yelling from Jeff when he can't get my attention.

He picks on me for the most mundane issues. For instance, he once screamed because I had the audacity to cut up the dog's treats on the same cutting board he was using to cut his spare ribs. Well, I thought he was done eating, and what's the big deal about a few dog treat crumbs?

Speaking of which, the thought of eating anything from a

pig disgusts me. One time we carried in Thai food (Don't tell the Chinese, but Jews have expanded their palates to other Asian countries.) and Jeff wanted to order Pad Thai with pork. "We're not having pork in this house," I exclaimed. He retorted, "Where do you think ribs come from? We carry in ribs all the time." Fair point, but ribs don't scream "pig" to me like ham and pork do.

In case you were wondering, this has nothing to do with religious beliefs. I haven't even eaten red meat since the 70s. When I went to school in Spain in 1975, all of the meat was hanging in the Charcuteria (Spanish butcher shop) and the sight of it made me ill. So for six months I had no red meat, and after returning home I decided that I didn't need it as part of my diet anyway.

Jeremy first discovered ham at my brother-in-law's house. I think Aunt Karen forgot that we didn't eat pork products and gave Jeremy a ham sandwich. He thought it was so tasty. Now, just to upset me, he orders ham in front of me every chance he gets, even from Zingerman's, a popular Jewish deli in Ann Arbor. What kind of person orders ham at a Jewish deli!?

I admit that if there are bacon bits in a salad, I'll choke them down, because bits are so bitty. (How could they really count?)

Filibuster

I never should have quit playing tennis. Tennis was one of the legacies passed down from my dad, and I was actually decent at it.

If I ever started playing again, I'm afraid I'd hurt my neck, my knees, twist my lower back, and injure other body parts that I can't even identify, so I'm stuck playing golf.

I've been taking golf lessons for a long time, and for the first five years or so, Jeff kept saying that I wasn't good enough to go out on the course.

Let me preface this by explaining that when I married Jeff, he led me to believe that he played golf maybe half a dozen times a year, due to his bad back. (Hah! Some bad back; it only flares up when he needs a convenient excuse.)

Rick had taken up golf when we dated, and I never had any interest. For some reason, I drive my husbands to golf. Better than driving them to drink! (Rick was never a big drinker, and Jeff didn't need the push.)

Anyway, the golf pro at our first club explained that he could keep taking my money, but I would never progress without actually playing. Still, Jeff insisted that I wasn't ready. Finally, my girlfriend said that she'd had enough of that attitude and dragged me out to play.

I never practice, but I always planned to improve by using the "think method" (similar to the method employed by Professor Harold Hill in *The Music Man*). Now on our second golf club, I'm still taking lessons and the "think method" hasn't worked out as well for me as it did for Robert Preston. The "think method" involved no practice or talent. The Harold Hill character (played by Robert Preston), out of laziness, and dishonesty instructed the band students to just "think" about the piece they were to play, and never actually taught them to read music.

My main goal at the golf lessons is to chat up the golf pros about their personal lives, share some stories, and make them laugh (which can be a challenge). The current pro at our club is a tough nut to crack. He is a very nice man, but he doesn't seem to be into chitchat, somehow preferring to teach me golf. Recently he instituted a policy that we had to save all conversation until after the lesson. (Right. He speeds off in his own golf cart the minute the lesson is over.)

He told me to stop making the excuse that I don't improve because I never practice, and that I have real potential. Personally, I'm afraid that if I practice I'll use up all of my good shots. Then what excuse will I have?

I can see why Jews were historically banned from country clubs. First of all, it can get very hot during golf, so right away I complain that I'm shvitzing. Then I chomp the ground with the club, which results in a shooting pain up my arm. Then I hit a horrible shot, which activates my tourettes, and swearing is not allowed on golf courses. (Not to mention that all of the twisting is bad for sore necks, knees, lower backs, etc.)

Universal truth #17: Jews complain constantly while golfing; gentiles stoically suck it up, play 18 holes, and appear to actually enjoy it.

Jews and Juicy Thighs

Universal Truth #18: Gentiles have thinner thighs than Jews.

My thighs would make very nice sofa cushions. My explanation for this phenomenon is that gentiles let their kids run freely, swim in lakes and oceans, and bike faster than at a snail's pace. Once my aunt and uncle took their grandkids to the ocean in Florida. We asked the kids if they enjoyed it, and they said that they weren't allowed to go in past the knees. Thus, the thighs get larger.

Also, gentile kids run around barefoot. This way the feet get bigger, which absorbs some of the fat away from the thighs. I studied my gentile nieces and their cousins. They all have long, lean, tan legs that look great as they walk around barefoot. They strike a pose while standing that strengthens the thigh muscles. Jews do not allow their kids to run around barefoot, as they might step on a piece of glass, a nail, or a rock, that would result in a catastrophic, formerly unknown, life-threatening illness (G-d forbid).

My Catholic nieces Angela and Shannon:
Longest legs ever

Jewish Parties

The moment I arrive at a party (okay, maybe after a bit of chatting), I start looking for the food. Jeff heads straight for the bar. At Jewish country clubs, the hors d'oeuvres and food lines are jammed. If you cut in, you do so at your own risk. There is no line at the bar, and it's harder for the clubs to make money.

I just returned from a wedding in Boca Raton (how Jews ended up in a city that means "Mouth Rat" is beyond me), and there was a cocktail hour after the ceremony. Although there was a small line at the bar (this was a Jewish drinking crowd), the hors d'oeuvres servers were attacked the minute they left the kitchen. (You would have thought people had been starving themselves for days!) The guests started lining up at the kitchen door, so they could attack the trays before the servers could even take a step. I was afraid the servers were going down, even at the hands of a crowd of thin, attractive people. One guest proclaimed that he went right into the kitchen to snatch an appealing scallop, rather than waiting to be served. This I have never seen at a gentile wedding.

Then there's the the dessert lines. I can't understand how the entire membership is on Atkins, or the Dukan Diet (the one that Kate Middleton's family went on before the big day), yet still fights to get to the dessert table.

When ordering salads, Jews always want them chopped. Chopping the salad is very important to Jews, and Jewish clubs and restaurants have caught on. So much so that there is now a designated salad chopper at every salad bar.

At a gentile club you can't get anywhere near the bar, although people do tend to wait patiently. I practically starved once during a luncheon at Oakland Hills Country Club. All of the food was hidden under cover of silver chafing dishes (kept warm by Sterno). You couldn't even see what the choices were. It was a "cocktail *two hours*." This club manager would not last at a Jewish club.

One thing I admire about Jewish country clubs is the requirement that members donate a certain amount to charity (usually a Jewish charity) before they are allowed to join. I think that almost all charities are worthy, but I believe that as Jews we have to take care of our own first.

Universal Truth #19: Gentile clubs are more profitable, due to larger liquor sales.

Jew or Not Jew?

Jews love a good famous person. We're well represented in Hollywood, but we are particularly proud of the few prominent Jewish professional athletes. In Detroit, we had Hank Greenberg and... okay, Hank Greenberg. (Jeff says that's it!) We'll ask, "Is he/she Jewish?" about everyone from somebody's date to a criminal on the news.

At a recent dinner, our friend mentioned that someone's forty year-old wife was having an affair with a twenty four year-old. My immediate response: "Is the guy Jewish?"

I was shocked to learn that Ringo Starr is not Jewish. As a huge Beatles fan, although Paul has always been my favorite, we all thought that Ringo (aka Richard Starkey) was Jewish. Turns out that the closest he came to tribe membership was marrying a half-Jew, but he didn't convert. Oh well.

The Madoff affair was horrible for us. Once it became public, after the initial outrage, you could hear the whisperings: "It had to be a Jew? Oy."

We are very defensive about monetary offenses, thanks to the stereotype of the "money grubbing Jew." I never heard the expression "Jew down" until I started working, and my own secretary was the one who used it (obviously without thinking). Gevult!

Collective Guilt

I have always been obsessed with the Holocaust. I did not have any close relatives that perished, but I knew of so many who did. We began learning about the horrors of World War II from a very early age in Hebrew school. Even as a young child, I could not fathom that the supposedly civilized German society could be convinced by a maniac to become accessories to the murder of eleven million people in an attempt to rid the world of Jews and other non-Aryans. These people committed atrocities beyond belief, including murdering over one million children.

I never tire of reading books on the Holocaust, both fiction and non-fiction. When I first worked at Jeff's law firm, if anyone found a book with a swastika on it, they knew it was mine. To this day, I still read books on the Holocaust and am still shocked to find myself learning of some previously unknown horror.

I had a distant relative named Herschel whom my Grandpa Louis helped move to Detroit. There was a scar on the back of his neck in the shape of an "X." When we asked him about it, Herschel explained that one night, the Nazi guards were bored and decided to play "tic, tac, toe" on people's bodies.

I very much respect Steven Spielberg for producing and

directing *Schindler's List*, and for creating an oral history project to document people's stories while the survivors are still alive.

When it comes to both the Holocaust and Israel, my kids tune me out. Much the way kids do when parents instruct them not to smoke, to look before crossing the street, etc.

Astoundingly, these atrocities were perpetrated a mere 60+ years ago, which historically speaking is hardly a blip.

I understand that there are atrocities perpetrated in the world to this day (in Sudan, Darfur...) and my heart aches for every murdered soul.

One can only imagine how difficult it is for many Jews to travel to Germany and/or Austria. I felt antipathy toward the Austrians when I visited. Our tour guide pointed out where Hitler made speeches. It made me sick. I unsuccessfully tried to envision the Von Trapps, to see if I could make the "hills come alive." I even tried humming *Edelweiss* continuously, but nothing helped.

Each time I met an Austrian, I wondered if they would have hidden us during the war.

However, when we visited Berlin, I was quite impressed. Berlin is a progressive city. The tour guides were sensitive to the fact that there we were Americans. The Holocaust Memorial Center is located on prime real estate in Berlin. Not that I'd pick up and move there, but unlike the Austrians, I respected their post-war perspective.

Universal Truth #20: Human beings are capable of perpetrating horrible evils, and we should NEVER FORGET.

Giants in the Netherlands

Jeff belongs to an international networking group of attorneys. I absolutely love spending time with these people. The attorneys and their spouses come from all over the world. The law firms take turns hosting, and we've traveled to many exciting locales. Frankly, I could be with this group in my backyard and love it.

One of my closest friends in the group is from the Netherlands, and he's the tallest one there at around 6 foot 8. To compensate for our size discrepancy, we developed a better way of communicating: When possible, he'll stand ten steps below me, making us nearly the same height. Otherwise, speaking to all of the Dutch lawyers (they just had to be my favorites) is a literal pain in the neck.

When the conference was in Amsterdam, I was the shortest person in the entire country. Not to mention that the Dutch are a hardy group, riding bicycles everywhere (and not the kind of bicycles with gears to make the pedaling easier). I'm convinced that all that biking in the fresh air makes them even taller. Even the cows look happier in the Netherlands.

When the conference was in China, Jeff flew home first class while I sat back in coach. In all fairness, Jeff is a foot taller than I am. However, men who are raised Jewish know to give the first class seat to their spouse. My stepfather Jack is more than a foot taller than my mom and would always insist she take the roomier seat.

If you hadn't guessed, the flight to China is very long. And do you think that my husband came back to check on me periodically, or even offered to split time in first class? More than twelve hours into the thirteen hour flight, he got up to stretch his legs, and he graced me with his presence (since he was up anyway). Obviously, by then I had everyone in the surrounding ten rows all in a huff about the maltreatment. The minute he walked back, I alerted my neighbors. The kind Indian gentleman next to me piped up: "Oh, so mister first class finally came to check on his wife. How considerate of you." Jeff, not being one to take abuse, skedaddled back in front of the dividing curtain as quickly as possible.

Recently, Jeff and I went to Brussels with the international legal group. We landed in Amsterdam and took a train the rest of the way. Which would have been a great plan for people who don't have hot flashes. We patiently waited for the train, and then BAM! All of the passengers tried to board with their luggage at once.

I had a big suitcase, a carry-on, my purse, and my Lululemon raincoat. As I attempted to get on the train, my raincoat fell in between the platform and the tracks. I could see it, but I couldn't reach it. My arms weren't long enough, Jeff's arms weren't long enough, and it's my favorite raincoat (plus I didn't have another coat with me). So, the train doors were closing and we had to get on without the coat. Trying to retrieve it wasn't quite worth being crushed by the train.

After we boarded, while I was in a semi-hysterical state, Jeff asked why I wasn't just wearing the coat (since it would have been one less thing to carry). Well, as he could have guessed, *I was having a hot flash!* (Honestly, men just don't understand these things.) We explained the situation to the train manager, who, after a series of complicated negotiations, arranged to have the coat transported on the next train to Brussels.

We waited around the Brussels train station for three hours (after having been up all night) and, miraculously, I found the one person on the next train who knew where it was. The tracks in Amsterdam are so clean that the coat remained in mint condition. For tall people, the Dutch are quite an agreeable bunch.

I always travel with a neck pillow for the plane ride and the hotel room (more support for my neck, since I'm always straining it looking up at people). On a girls' trip to Florida, I inadvertently left the neck pillow on the hotel bed and didn't notice that it was missing until it was almost midnight. I was rooming with my friend Marcy, who is very organized and usually very relaxed, but needs her sleep.

Once I realized that the pillow was gone, I called housekeeping to see if by any chance they'd found it. Little did I know that they would send out the cavalry to try to track it down. A detective asked for a description of the stolen item, and I patiently explained that I didn't think it was stolen, just mixed up with the linens.

I had to answer around 50 questions. By the time he asked me for the value (twelve dollars) Marcy was ready to murder me. She actually said she was going to murder me. Well, thanks to menopause, I was in an extremely sensitive state, and after she said she wouldn't room with me again, I got a bit weepy (for three hours, actually). We made up, and now we laugh about it, but I still don't understand why a hotel would feel the need to send their version of the FBI to track down a neck pillow.

Our Nation's Capital

I absolutely love Washington DC. Hilary just completed her master's degree in nurse anesthesia at Georgetown. During the two and a half year program, I'd go visit and stay with my dear friend Ilene who lives there. It was a big relief for me knowing that Ilene was there for Hilary. She adopted her as her own for the entire program.

The week before Hilary moved to DC, I tripped while leaving the house in clogs and broke my ankle. Well, there was no way she was moving to DC without my help (so said I). I begged the orthopod to let me go. He reluctantly agreed with the stipulation that I not walk too much on the crutches (I had a cast up to my knee), so Hilary had to push me long distances in a travel wheelchair. I did end up mastering the crutches (except on stairs. where I went up and down on my butt).

We got her room furnished (crutches and all), and I had a blast using the motorized shopping carts in Target and Bed Bath and Beyond. Taking corners without knocking over a display or two was a bit challenging, but all-in-all I think we were a great team.

Naturally, Hilary was a bit nervous to take on a new city and start a difficult program. If we went more than a block, she had to push me in the wheelchair in 102 degree humid weather. I'm not sure what she was muttering under her breath, but after all, she is a nurse. She took an oath!

Jeff always accuses me of imposing on people. He thinks I have no shame. Hil and I stayed with Ilene and her family in DC (with me doing the butt crawl on the stairs) for one week. I called an old boyfriend to ask if his son could help put up some cabinets in Hilary's room. I don't think his wife really appreciated it, but we needed help! Hey, I'm always willing to help if asked.

Universal Truth #21: Jews have no shame and readily ask for favors; gentiles try to do everything themselves.

Ilene loves to plan fun activities when I come to visit. During Hilary's first summer in DC, Ilene organized a fun, one way, nine mile bike ride with our girls to Mt. Vernon. We were going to return by ferry. We arrived at the bike rental store a bit late, so by the time we left, it was past noon. When we started the ride, the temperature was a balmy 99 degrees. (I don't understand how people can even wear clothes in DC during the summer.)

I had not been on a bike for years, and cardio is not my thing (I stick to Pilates). Ilene and the girls quickly passed me by. I was huffing and puffing, and I had to get off the bike every few blocks to bend over and catch my breath. Sweat was pouring down my body. I thought it might be the end. I texted Jeff, "Mile 4, nice knowing you," and he texted back: "Get a cab, seriously." That's all I needed to keep going.

Having been abandoned by my group, I made friends with

three other slow riders: Aisha, Rodney and Brent.

After two hours, Ilene had no idea where I was, so she headed back to look for me. (By this time, even Aisha, Rodney and Brent had reluctantly dropped me.) After several inquiries, she encountered Brent and Aisha. "Did you happen to see a blond woman struggling on the trail?"

"Yes."

"Is she okay? We tried to call her, but she didn't answer."

"Oh yeah, we saw her all right, and she doesn't want to talk to any of you." (My own daughter had left me for dead on a treacherous, broilingly hot bike trail!)

Ingeniously, I managed to rope a nice family into loading my bike on their Suburban and driving me the last mile up to Mt. Vernon (it was all uphill).

When I finally reunited with the girls, I played it cool (and naturally gave Hilary the silent treatment for a few hours). Ilene explained that she'd run into some people who saw me, and I excitedly exclaimed: "Oh. You saw, Aisha, Brent, and Rodney?" (I'd love to see them again, to express my thanks for keeping me company.)

After riding nine miles back on the return (alone, of course, but at least it was downhill), I actually clocked 18 miles that day. (Okay, seventeen if you don't count the mile I hitchhiked.)

Universal Truth #22: Biking 18 (17) miles in humid 102 degree heat is an awful idea if you're not a professional bicyclist.

Overnight Camp

For some reason, a disproportionate number of Jewish kids go to overnight camp. And it can be a wonderful experience, for those who don't suffer from homesickness.

My first camp experience came at age nine and lasted three weeks. I wrote my parents every day begging them to bring me home. I very dramatically explained that I wasn't eating and that I was crying into my pillow every night when the other kids couldn't see. My parents wrote me every day, but they wouldn't come take me home. Now I'm glad they made me stay, since it certainly helped build character.

On the last day of camp, the camp director called me over after flagpole and said, "I heard you've been very homesick." (Ya think?) He was a bit slow on the uptake.

The next summer, my parents thought that we should try a non-cliquey, ecumenical camp. The popular physical education teacher from my elementary school had a camp in northern Michigan that seemed to fit the bill. He came to our house and showed us slides. So off I went to this six week camp. I signed up for riding four times a week. The first time I got on the horse, I was petrified and quit riding. I was more homesick than ever.

I had perfected the art of pleading to come home the

previous summer. This time I wrote and told my mom that I'd saved the piece of Kleenex she gave me at the bus and cried into it every night. (You should have seen it by week six.) My mom said that she dreaded getting the mail every day. She saved the letters for years, in case she needed to blackmail me or something.

My family came for visiting day, but instead of touring all of the fun activities the camp had to offer, I cried the entire time and begged them to take me home. Again, I ended up staying. I'm still glad, because I actually have very fond memories of camp. But the camp director didn't want me around the younger campers, for fear that my homesickness might be contagious.

Finally, by my third year at camp (at age twelve) I stopped crying. The homesickness was under control. I had a big part in the camp play. It was great.

Thank goodness Jeremy and Hilary were much better campers than I was. I always got nervous before they left for camp, but I truly believe that camp was a wonderful experience for them.

Universal Truth #23: Jews send their kids to overnight camp; gentile kids spend the summer participating in sports, which in turn keeps their thighs thin.

Anonymous

There is no such thing as anonymity with Jews. Enter any building in our community and every doorway, door knob, sink, toilet, floor and ceiling has been donated by someone.

The West Bloomfield Jewish Community Center (JCC) is a wonderful facility. Sometimes multiple families contribute to an area, such as a social hall. When this happens, the organization needs to creatively appease both families. In this event, there is usually a room divider to split the room in half so that both groups have a nicely sized dedication plaque. (And there's probably a dedication for the room divider as well.)

Israel is a country full of dedications. Even approaching the ancient Western Wall in Jerusalem, there is the William Davidson plaque commemorating his contribution to excavating the area.

Reverse Discrimination

Ironically, my kids have always had many non-Jewish friends. As with many ethnic groups, there is a certain element in Jewish society that thinks the Jews are better than everyone else. (What would you expect from a group dubbed "The Chosen People?")

This reverse discrimination is not good for us. All of my Grandpa Louis' grandchildren eventually married gentiles, the majority of whom converted. Two of us divorced our first Jewish spouses. Some people in the Jewish community thought that this was shameful (a "shanda"). The truth is that although we were raised with strong Jewish values, we were also raised to judge people for their core values. This created a true double standard.

I struggle eternally with this concept. I would love my kids to marry someone Jewish, but I will certainly support them if they choose not to do so. Of course, I hope that they'll raise their kids with some Jewish affiliation.

Judaism allows more room for interpretation than other mainstream religions. A reform Jew can feel just as committed and involved as an orthodox Jew; it just boils down to their personal interpretation of our laws and traditions.

I have tremendous respect for our Jewish traditions, and I

hope that my kids have absorbed some of my enthusiasm. My approach with them has always leaned more toward honoring customs rather than preaching religious tenets. I understand that parents can not force religion on their adult children. They should only be healthy!

Jewish weddings end with the groom stomping on a glass (or light bulb for easier breakage and a bigger pop), then everyone yells "Mazel tov!" There are several interpretations of this tradition. It is suggested that joy always be tempered with sorrow, or that even in times of celebration the Jews should remember the destruction of the Temple in Jerusalem. This is a beautiful tradition, and when I'm at a gentile wedding, I always feel like something is missing without a good smash and a cheer.

The kids and I were in *Fiddler on the Roof* together. After seeing the production (again, my 88 year-old aunt thought I was going to Broadway), my uncle the historian explained that our family history was similar to the one portrayed in the play. We hailed from a tailor, a butcher and a scholar, and everyone had to leave Russia to escape the pogroms.

Retail? Never!

Jeff has no patience for bargaining. He thinks his time is too valuable to look for a better deal. (He must not have dunked himself long enough in the mikvah at the conversion ceremony.)

He doesn't even ask for senior tickets at the movies. *WHAT KIND OF PERSON DOESN'T ASK FOR SENIOR TICKETS WHEN THEY'RE OVER 70?!* On this alone, he would prove himself a gentile if the Nazis invaded our state (G-d forbid). They'll probably hide at the ticket counter to see who asks for a discount.

He doesn't review the Visa bill carefully. Even worse, he doesn't check the bill at restaurants to be sure that we weren't erroneously charged for an extra beverage or meal. *WHAT KIND OF PERSON DOESN'T REVIEW A RESTAURANT BILL WITH A FINE-TOOTH COMB?!*

He's also not so great at asking for favors. I have no such shame. Jeff claims that he'll ask for the favor, but he can't go through with it (gentile breeding).

In the writing of this memoir alone, I've had to enlist the help of my friends the Nosans on several occasions. Late one evening I thought I had deleted the entire manuscript. It was past ten, and Jeff would never bother someone at that hour. I called, for probably the tenth time that week, ran over there, and sure enough Terry (one of the family's many computer and printer experts) was able to find it for me. If I call and they don't answer, I always worry that they're screening my calls, but so far they've been very good sports about being my personal tech support.

The Experts

Every good Jew has friends they can call for the following: Health matters (every specialty), legal matters, computer issues, heating and cooling, and construction repairs. This means that we can call our "people" in these areas any time between the hours of 6:00 am and midnight.

To be so bold as to mention that you went to someone out of the "recommended network" is to invite a tirade explaining the stupidity of taking such an action. I have certain friends whom I call for a recommendation in any of the above mentioned areas. Why reinvent the wheel? If I fail to follow their advice, I'll just have to waste time switching to a different specialist, or returning a printer or barbecue. It's just too much trouble!

Universal Truth #24: Jews must be convinced that they are not paying retail prices, and must have experts on hand for every possible eventuality. Gentiles will pay full price, and will go to a specialist recommended by their physician, without having to run it by the "network brigade."

Enunciate

One way to try and pass as a gentile for a few minutes is to drop the "g" at the end of words. Jeff will still default to this habit when surrounded by non-Jews. "Are you goin' to the game?" "The Tigers are not playin' too well." I can't quite identify how this evolved, but I have a theory:

Quite often, I notice the "g" dropping when there is beer around. I think the bitterness of the beer affects the uvula in the throat, causing a softening of the "g." I also notice people dropping their g's when standing for cocktails, especially guys who have a beer in one hand (with the other in the pocket of their navy blazer).

In further support of my theory, I've noticed that some orthodox Jews tend to over-pronounce the "g." No beer, no softening of the uvula, and out comes a hard "g."

Emoticons

Finally, an invention to succinctly portray my enthusiasm and opinions on any number of subjects! Since I discovered emoticons, seldom do I write a text or email without them. For all of my Jewish organizational work, there is a Jewish star emoticon. For literacy related activity, there are books. For friends and family, I sign off with multiple hearts. Want to go to coffee? There is an emoticon for a cup of coffee. I just love them!

iTunes

The only invention better than emoticons is iTunes. I love music, and as soon as I realized that I could download just one song from an album, I was in second heaven. I can't tell you how many CDs I've bought where I only liked one or two songs.

Typically, when I hear a song I like, I must have it identified ASAP so that I can purchase it on iTunes immediately and proceed to listen to it a hundred times in a row.

If I'm out and hear a song I love, I use an app called Shazam that can identify songs within hearing distance of your cell phone. (Of course this is assuming I can remember the name of the app, which is an unfortunate challenge for me. It usually dawns on me after the song has already ended.) If I've missed my chance with the Shazam app, Plan B is to call and leave a humming voicemail for Hilary, who can identify it for me nine times out of ten.

I have a wide selection of genres on my iPod: Broadway musicals, Hebrew songs, Spanish songs, French songs, songs from Glee, songs from *When Harry Met Sally* and other romantic comedies, mournful melodies from more serious films, songs from commercials, and many more.

Listening to music can be very cathartic for me. A few notes from a meaningful song and I am instantly transported to the era when I first heard it.

Trauma at the Car Wash

I love the drive-through car wash. I always vacuum my car thoroughly beforehand, so I don't have to pay for the full service (that would be too much like paying retail). And after paying, I get the fabulous thick wipes to clean out the interior. As it turns out, this can be a hazard.

Not long ago I was diligently wiping off the interior, paying special attention to the steering wheel, when all of a sudden my car jumped right off the track. I was startled, and then the idiot behind me smashed into my car. That part wasn't his fault, as we were all on the assembly line, but he started honking at me like crazy. Then, after they got us all pulled over (having shut down the track) the idiot and his young wife started screaming and swearing at me, like it was my fault! I asked the car wash manager to call the police, and I called my son at work (I don't usually bother him at work) crying because the idiot would not stop yelling at me. I didn't think I did anything wrong, and even if I somehow did, it was an accident!

Eventually Jeff showed up (he never shows up fast enough in emergencies, plus he can't stand it when I'm overly emotional). The policeman took all of the pertinent info and was extremely solicitous of me in my sobbing state, but my hysterics were genuine. And what kind of idiot wife goes along with her idiot husband when he's obviously in a blind rage? The car wash manager apologized for even letting him near me and said if he had realized that the man was screaming at me, he would have sent someone to intervene.

Upon returning home, I did what any good Jewish person would do: I called the car wash owner at his home. I knew his wife, but I'd only met him once. He handled it very well. I explained that I was afraid that the idiot might file a lawsuit (or take some other drastic action) since he was foaming at the mouth.

I also explained that I thought the car may have just jumped off of the track due to some defect. He very patiently explained that the only way a car can jump off the track is by touching the brake, or turning the steering wheel. I didn't think I'd done either, but I harbored a nagging doubt about the steering wheel, since I *was* cleaning it.

Luckily, the idiot never sued. From the police report I saw that he actually worked at one of the local temples. (With a temper like that?) Naturally, I called someone who was on the temple board to explain the fiasco. He concurred that the idiot had some anger management issues and asked me if I wanted him to lose his job.

What I wanted was justice, and an apology, but I did not want to be responsible for him losing his job, so I let it go. I am now extra careful when I'm at the car wash, and I always wipe off the steering wheel before I get on the track.

Universal Truth #25: It is dangerous to use cleaning wipes at the car wash while the car is on the track.

Happy Holidays

In addition to working as a probate paralegal, I also worked as the office administrator (COO). This was a challenging and mostly rewarding position, but the human resources portion could be daunting. The following is one of my favorite email chains that best captures the essence of a job that involves catering to the needs of a diverse office population:

FROM: Pat Lewis, Human Resources Director

DATE: December 1

RE: Christmas Party

I'm happy to inform you that the company Christmas Party will take place on December 23, starting at noon in the banquet room at Luigi's Open Pit Barbecue. No-host bar, but plenty of eggnog! We'll have a small band playing traditional carols... feel free to sing along. And don't be surprised if our CEO shows up dressed as Santa Claus!

FROM: Pat Lewis, Human Resources Director

DATE: December 2

RE: Christmas Party

In no way was yesterday's memo intended to exclude our Jewish employees. We recognize that Chanukah is an important holiday which often coincides with Christmas, though unfortunately not this year. However, from now on we're calling it our "Holiday Party." The same policy applies to employees who are celebrating Kwanzaa at this time. Happy now?

FROM: Pat Lewis, Human Resources Director

DATE: December 3

RE: Holiday Party

Regarding the note I received from a member of Alcoholics Anonymous requesting a non-drinking table... you didn't sign your name. I'm happy to accommodate this request, but if I put a sign on a table that reads, "AA Only" you wouldn't be anonymous anymore. How am I supposed to handle this? Somebody?

FROM: Pat Lewis, Human Resources Director

DATE: December 7

RE: Holiday Party

What a diverse company we are! I had no idea that December 20 begins the Muslim holy month of Ramadan, which forbids eating, drinking and sex during daylight hours. There goes the party! Seriously, we can appreciate how a luncheon this time of year does not accommodate our Muslim employees' beliefs. Perhaps Luigi's can hold off on serving your meal until the end of the party—the days are so short this time of year or else package everything for take-home in little foil swans. Will that work? Meanwhile, I've arranged for members of Overeaters Anonymous to sit farthest from the dessert buffet and pregnant women will get the table closest to the restrooms.

Did I miss anything?

FROM: Pat Lewis, Human Resources Director

DATE: December 8

RE: Holiday Party

So December 22 marks the Winter Solstice...what do you expect me to do, a tap-dance on your heads? Fire regulations at Luigi's prohibit the burning of sage by our "earth-based Goddess-worshipping" employees, but we'll try to accommodate your shamanic drumming circle during the band's breaks. Okay???

FROM: Pat Lewis, Human Resources Director

DATE: December 9

RE: Holiday Party

People, people, nothing sinister was intended by having our CEO dress up like Santa Claus! Even if the anagram of "Santa" does happen to be "Satan," there is no evil connotation to our own "little man in a red suit." It's a tradition, folks, like sugar shock at Halloween or family feuds over the Thanksgiving turkey or broken hearts on Valentine's Day. Could we lighten up?

FROM: Pat Lewis, Human Resources Director

DATE: December 10

RE: Holiday Party

Vegetarians!?!?!? I've had it with you people!!! We're going to keep this party at Luigi's Open Pit Barbecue whether you like it or not, so you can sit quietly at the table furthest from the "grill of death," as you so quaintly put it, and you'll get your #$%^&*! salad bar, including hydroponic tomatoes. But you know, they have feelings, too. Tomatoes scream when you slice them. I've heard them scream. I'm hearing them scream right now!

FROM: Teri Bishops, Acting Human Resources Director

DATE: December 14

RE: Pat Lewis and Holiday Party

I'm sure I speak for all of us in wishing Pat Lewis a speedy recovery from her stress-related illness and I'll continue to forward your cards to her at the sanitarium. In the meantime, management has decided to cancel our Holiday Party and give everyone the afternoon of the 23rd off with full pay.

Scrooge

I hate Christmas and New Year's. I never liked this time of the year, and when my dad died the day after Christmas, that clinched it.

First of all, the days are depressingly short since it gets dark so early. Secondly, many radios start playing Christmas music immediately after Halloween. "It's the Most Wonderful Time of the Year?" Are they crazy?! The malls are packed, no parking spaces available, Christmas music playing nonstop in the background, blinding red and green decorations, and the line to see Santa is miles long! There's so much phony cheer, and it's not even my holiday. There's no surer way to feel like an outsider in your own country than not to celebrate Christmas.

I find buying gifts for at least fifty people very stressful. It's a never-ending process. From the postal workers to office staff, everyone gets a gift. Plus, I never worked in a field where I was on the receiving end of all of this joy.

When I ran the law firm, I was in charge of selecting the client holiday cards (very difficult with Jewish partners) with a nice holiday-but-not-too-Christmassy theme. Then the attorneys and I selected gifts for the staff, and we nearly went broke shopping for 20 people. I do love it when people enjoy the gifts I give, but it's still stressful.

I believe in giving to those in need, and that it is better to give than to receive. However, during Christmas, the hairdressers in the salon make out like bandits, receiving more designer swag than that year's Oscar attendees. Somehow, the act of giving in this circumstance just doesn't feel as meaningful.

I get depressed from the day after Thanksgiving to the first of January. The only thing I hate worse than Christmas is New Year's Eve. So much forced joviality and pressure to have big plans. *I hate it.* I prefer to just get out of town and try to ignore the holiday season altogether.

Not to mention that people don't put out Christmas lights like they did in the old days. I've told my gentile neighbors that they're a major disappointment in the lights department, but this never seems to propel them into putting up more lights.

Gentile people very nicely wish me a happy Hanukkah in response to my wishing them a Merry Christmas, but Hanukkah isn't even a major Jewish holiday. Our most important holidays are Rosh Hashanah (the Jewish New Year) and Yom Kippur (our Day of Atonement). Hanukkah only rose to prominence because of its proximity to Christmas.

When possible, Jews try to go out of town during Christmas holidays. We used to go visit my in-laws in Apopka, Florida over Christmas when the kids were younger. Of course it made sense that their Jewish grandkids were the only ones who visited for Christmas. It was very relaxing, and I had my own handmade personalized stocking (a first!). I explained to the kids that we were celebrating their grandparents' holiday, and that this was not our holiday. We spent many years this way, and although I'm grateful to have had this special time with them, it was always a hard time for me. I missed my dad, and I was in a totally Christian environment for ten straight days. There was only one Jewish couple in the entire complex of over a thousand people. Also, the surrounding town was a bit depressing. No one getting hair blowouts, no Asian nail salons, no Pilates. I couldn't believe that Apopka and Boca were actually located in the same state.

Since my dad died right after Christmas, that's when his yahrzeit date typically falls. (It's not exact, since Jewish custom follows the lunar calendar.) Jewish tradition provides that on the Hebrew anniversary of an immediate family member's date of death, that the surviving relatives go to services to say the traditional mourning prayer (Kaddish, written in Aramaic). It is a time to reflect upon, and honor the memory of the deceased. There is a yahrzeit candle that burns for twenty four hours. It is very important to me that I go to services to say the memorial prayer, and that I light the yahrzeit candle.

Needless to say, there were no synagogues, bagels, or challah bread within a fifty mile radius of Apopka. Since Al Gore hadn't yet invented the internet, my mother-in-law made many phone calls to try to find a daily service for me to attend. Sometimes I drove an hour, but thanks to her kindness I was able to get there for my dad.

My mom also hates this time of the year. She says it's worse for her than me.

"Why, Mom?"

"I was in the hospital twice."

"That was hard for me too, Mom. I was very worried."

"Well, then Jack had serious surgery over Christmas."

"That was also hard for me, Mom."

Great, so it's a tie as to who suffers the most over the holidays. And you wonder how I ended up this way?

I've been tolerating all of the Christmas music a bit better since the release of *When Harry Met Sally* and *Love Actually*. Both feature Christmas songs, and sometimes I find myself humming along, thinking of romantic comedies.

Oddly enough, I love Christmas movies, even though I hate Christmas. If Jews are in town for Christmas, the tradition is to carry in Chinese food. If Christmas is "the most wonderful time of the year" for anyone, it's Chinese restaurateurs!

Universal Truth #26: Christmas is for Christians, and Chinese restaurateurs.

Mamma Mia

As I'm getting older, I find myself with so many friends who have lost one or both of their parents. As hard as it's been for me not to have my father around for the last 30 years, I have to say how grateful I am to still have my mother.

She's always been very devoted to me and the kids, and people always tell me that they think she is so sweet and pretty. And she is! Since I took up the furshtunkana game of bridge, my mom has offered to tutor our bridge group.

Two of the girls in our group have already lost their mothers and say that they only wish their mothers were still here. My mom is already 80, and I hope she has many more good years ahead of her. She (though I'm not supposed to refer to her as "she"—it's a generational thing) really wants at least one of my kids to get married soon, so that: 1. She'll still be around to see them happily married off; and 2. She'll have to go on a wedding diet, in order to be the svelte grandma at the wedding.

My mom was just in the hospital with an arm pain scare (everything turned out fine, thank goodness) and the nurses, techs and doctors all told her that she looked like she was 65. For this reason alone, she wasn't in a huge rush to leave.

My mom remarried a very nice man named Jack, who has

always been very devoted to all of us. He doesn't dare make a move without first checking with my mom, and they've already had 27 years of marital bliss together. He's the one who always took the kids to Toys R Us and McDonald's, and would have jumped off the roof if they asked him to.

Ask Jack where he's going: "I don't know, ask your mother."

Ask Jack how he's feeling: "I don't know, ask your mother."

Can you come for dinner tonight? Again, "Ask your mother."

Every day he makes my mom her iced tea, fills her car with gas, does the grocery shopping, the cooking, the laundry, you name it.

Once I unintentionally butt-dialed my mom. She usually can't hear me very well on the phone (she could really use a hearing aid but says they're too expensive), but she had no problem understanding me that time. I had run into some friends at Starbucks who asked me about her and Jack. I said they were fine, that they'd both had pneumonia, and that Jack was back to waiting on her hand and foot like a slave. How she could hear this from a butt call was miraculous.

I said to the friends, "Oops, I just butt-dialed my mom. I hope she didn't hear me."

Two seconds later the phone rang.

"I think you just butt-called me."

"I did. Sorry, Mom."

"I heard what you said!"

"There's no way you could have heard me with the phone in my purse."

"You said that Jack waits on me hand and foot like a slave. So as penance, please bring me an iced tea from Starbucks."

Recently, my mom and Jack were home with bad coughs, so I would call and cheer them up with interesting anecdotes.

I heard an interesting radio piece on the BBC (practicing my English accent) about a woman whose mother absolutely loved the television show *CSI*. My mother loves murder shows (going back to *Murder She Wrote*) and watches them for hours after she finishes reading *The New York Times*.

Anyway, the BBC piece reported that the *CSI* loving mother passed away. And since she was such a huge fan, her daughter contacted the producers of the show and offered her mother's body to play a murdered corpse, using the deceased's real first name.

I thought that my mother would find this entertaining. I called to relay the story, and let's just say it didn't yield the desired result. After sharing the details:

"Why are you telling me this?"

"I thought you'd find it entertaining, especially since you're such a *CSI* fan."

"I don't watch *CSI*, I watch *Criminal Minds*."

"Sorry, Mom. I can't keep your murder shows straight."

"And don't get any ideas."

In her defense, she was a bit cranky from having been cooped up with a cough, but did my mom really think I was going to offer up her G-d forbid dead body to the producers of *CSI* or *Criminal Minds*?

Ever since I put down our dog Maggy (shortly after a lymphoma diagnosis, so she wouldn't suffer) my mom thinks I'm some kind of hasty-decision-making Dr. Death and doesn't trust me to make responsible decisions as it relates to these things.

Universal Truth #27: There is nothing like a mother's love.

My mom and me (Isn't she adorable?)

Jeff, Hil, my mom and Jack at
Meggie Wolf's gorgeous wedding (2012)

(1) First game under the lights at Michigan Stadium (The Big
House) to beat Notre Dame! (2011)

(2) Michigan Basketball Bar in Chicago (MOST EXCITING
BASKETBALL GAME EVER. Trey Burke hit a 3 pointer to put
us into overtime. The whole place went crazy.)

MEECHIGAN Football game with Jeremy (in my dad's hat), Jeff (not quite smiling), Hilary with a beer, and three of Jeremy's best law school friends.

Pros and Cons

My mother keeps asking me where I think I'm going with this memoir. (A very good question.) I told her that someone has to succeed in these endeavors!

This story is not meant to be a "Jew versus Gentile" rant. There will never be world peace until people learn to accept and respect those whose beliefs are different than their own.

Millions have been killed in the name of religion. I find it noteworthy that there has never been a Jewish version of the Inquisition or Crusades. (At worst, we might forget to offer a gentile guest a drink.)

The truth is that I love and respect my religion, and our accompanying traditions. Jews are taught to analyze and debate holy teachings. This distinguishes Judaism from many other religions that are based on dogma, with very strict guidelines to follow.

Maybe this is why Jews tend to be so verbal, and appear to question almost everything, especially portion sizes. A typical discussion:

"How was the restaurant?"

"The food went downhill, and the portions were so small."

Many gentiles have alcohol issues.

Many Jews are neurotic.

Of course, as intermarriage becomes more prevalent, we see a mishmash of cultures, and soon there will be neurotic gentiles with blossoming thighs married to drinking Jews.

I truly wish the best for everyone. Maybe my kids will help keep Jewish traditions going, even if they end up marrying a gentile (or G-d forbid they would end up alone). One can only hope. Hover no more! Give them roots and give them wings!

Periods at the ends of my sentences.

It's not important to always have the last word.

Remember to breathe, stop interrupting.

L'chaim! and GO BLUE!

ACKNOWLEDGMENTS

I'd like to thank my wonderful children, Jeremy and Hilary, whom I couldn't love more, but who are so sick of my stories that they had no interest in helping me with this memoir. I'd like to thank my husband Jeff, who after reading two pages offered the priceless advice that I'd used too many semicolons (;;;;;) then stopped reading. I am very grateful to my wonderful, adorable Mom Selma and her devoted husband Jack, who is a very nice stepfather and Papa. Dad, I hope you've got a Kindle up there. I'll never stop loving or missing you. Amy Beth Dishell, this is also for you, I miss you every day. I'd like to thank Auntie Barbara and Uncle Harold for being like second parents to me. Many thanks to my friends and their kids that read this in advance and encouraged me to continue writing. I'd like to thank my closest friends and family; you know who you are. You are thoughtful, supportive, devoted, patient, and I love you all. To my Israeli friends, who have opened their hearts and homes to me, you are also my family.

Made in the USA
Charleston, SC
20 October 2013